to
Emily Brontë's

Wuthering
Heights

---

by
Graham Bradshaw

Contents

NOTES

Introduction

Wuthering Heights is one of the most written-about novels in the English language. Famous for the dark and passionate world Emily Brontë creates, and for the doomed relationship between Catherine Earnshaw and Heathcliff, it is a story which has almost become synonymous with romance, not just for Hollywood, chick lit writers and advertisers but for many who have read it and many more who haven't. Countless stories, films, television adaptations and magazine articles owe their origins or inspiration to Brontë's extraordinary story of love and death in the Yorkshire moors. Catherine's desperate avowal – "Nelly, I *am* Heathcliff" – has been described as the most romantic sentence in fiction.

For all its later enormous influence and reputation, the novel had relatively little impact in the first 50 years or so after publication. It was easily eclipsed in fame and critical renown by *Jane Eyre*, the more straightforwardly romantic novel written by Emily's sister, Charlotte, and the runaway bestseller of 1847. It wasn't until the early 20th century that critical opinion began to change, and that change owed a great deal to the formidable critic Mrs Humphry Ward, who lavished *Wuthering Heights* with praise in her introduction to the Haworth edition of the works of the Brontë sisters. Ward thought Emily Brontë a greater writer than her sister – a view later reinforced by the critic David Cecil in what is undoubtedly the most powerful essay of his *Early Victorian Novelists* (1934). Critical momentum steadily grew after this and in recent years the novel has been all but overwhelmed in a flood of criticism of all kinds, with Marxists, feminists and psychoanalysts all finding plenty of grist for their particular mills.

So what is *Wuthering Heights* really about? Is it the Great Romantic Novel which so many readers, critics and film-makers assume it to be? What are we meant to make of Heathcliff, the lonely, violent man at the heart of Brontë's story? Why is *Wuthering Heights* open to so many different interpretations, as Frank Kermode believes it is (though he sees this as a sign of its greatness)? In this book I will explore these questions and attempt to show why Emily Brontë's novel remains such a vivid, subtle and resonant work more than 150 years after it was first published.

A summary of the plot

The novel begins in 1801. Mr Lockwood, a gentleman from the south of England – and one of the two main narrators – has rented a house in Yorkshire called Thrushcross Grange. Soon after his arrival he visits his landlord, Mr Heathcliff, who lives in a remote moorland farmhouse called

Wuthering Heights, and despite an unfriendly reception ends up staying the night. Lockwood has a nightmare followed by something much more disturbing: the appearance at the window of a sobbing child; she announces herself as Catherine Linton who has been "a waif for twenty years". The child terrifies Lockwood and – "terror made me cruel" – he rubs her wrist on the broken glass. Lockwood's screams bring Heathcliff, who flies into a monstrous rage on learning of the nightmare (if that is what it is) and is later overheard by Lockwood beseeching Catherine at the open window to come to him. Lockwood returns exhausted to Thrushcross Grange where he is tended by the housekeeper, Nelly Dean.

Nelly is persuaded to amuse him by telling him the story of the Earnshaws, the Lintons and the Heathcliffs. Her tale begins 30 years earlier, in the summer of 1771. (As C. P. Sanger famously showed, the novel's chronology is very carefully worked out.) Mr Earnshaw, the owner of the Heights, leaves to visit Liverpool (he says) and promises to bring back presents for his two children, a fiddle for Hindley and a whip for Catherine. In fact, what he brings back is "a dirty, ragged, black-haired child", found abandoned (he says) in the streets of the city. He is christened "Heathcliff" which serves him for both Christian name and surname.

The arrival of Heathcliff has a disastrous effect.

Hindley, barely 14, is supplanted in his father's affections by the mysterious foundling. At the same time Heathcliff develops a passionate natural kinship with Catherine, then six. Because of the discord Hindley is sent away to college, but returns three years later – when Mr Earnshaw dies – having married a southern girl named Frances. As the new master of the Heights, he forces Heathcliff to become a servant, and Heathcliff is regularly beaten by Hindley and by the "vinegar-faced" old retainer, Joseph.

A few months later Heathcliff and Catherine go to Thrushcross Grange to spy on the Linton family who live there. They are spotted, and when they try to escape Catherine is viciously mauled by a dog. She is brought inside the Grange to have her injuries tended; Heathcliff is sent home. When she eventually returns to the Heights, dressed in new clothes, she looks and acts like a lady and laughs at Heathcliff's unkempt appearance. Degraded by Hindley and deeply hurt by Catherine's growing affection for Edgar Linton, Heathcliff runs away.

By the time he returns, in September 1783, Hindley's wife Frances has died (after giving birth to a son, Hareton) and Catherine has been married to Edgar for five months. Her love for Edgar, she tells Nelly, is the kind of love that is bound to change, "like the foliage in the woods", while the love she feels for Heathcliff "resembles the eternal rocks beneath".

During his period away Heathcliff has become rich, though it is never clear how, educated and self-confident – he now has a "half-civilised ferocity". Re-establishing contact with Catherine, he asserts his claims over her and the resulting disruption of the Thrushcross Grange household and strain on Catherine leads to her death, aged only 19 (and after giving birth to a daughter, Catherine), in March 1784. Meanwhile, Isabella Linton, Edgar's sister, has become infatuated with Heathcliff and Heathcliff – determined to take revenge not just on Hindley but on the Linton family too – makes her his wife in a runaway marriage as part of a plan to get possession of Thrushcross Grange.

The rest of the novel revolves around Heathcliff's plan for revenge. He succeeds in marrying his own weak and effeminate son, Linton, to the younger Catherine in August 1801. (Linton is the product of his marriage to Isabella, before, bruised and miserable after her sadistic treatment, she runs away from him.) But Linton is already dying and survives for less than two months after the marriage. As a result Heathcliff now manages to get all the Linton property into his hands, Edgar Linton also having died.* By now Heathcliff has also succeeded in destroying Hindley, who has drunk himself to death in September 1884, though

*In a carefully researched essay in 1926, C.P. Sanger argues that in fact Heathcliff's legal title to Thrushcross Grange is very dubious. Sanger's essay can still be read on the web.

John Sutherland argues in his essay, "Is Heathcliff a murderer?", that Heathcliff could have prevented the death but didn't, in effect killing him. As for Hareton, Hindley's son – Heathcliff tries to degrade him into an uncouth and illiterate servant.

Heathcliff's obsession, however, has remained the dead Catherine, with whom he steadfastly believes he will be reunited. We have now come back to the point where the novel opens, and when Lockwood sees Catherine at the window, Heathcliff believes she has returned to him at last. He gives up his plans for revenge, ceases to eat and dies in what David Daiches calls "an ecstasy of expectation of reunion with Catherine". Meanwhile, the young Catherine softens and educates Hareton Earnshaw until he becomes civilised enough to marry her. So the wheel has come full circle: the novel ends, as it begins, with a Catherine Earnshaw.

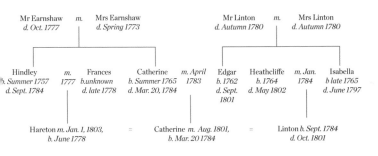

| Mr Earnshaw
d. Oct. 1777 | *m.* | Mrs Earnshaw
d. Spring 1773 | | | Mr Linton
d. Autumn 1780 | *m.* | Mrs Linton
d. Autumn 1780 |

| Hindley
b. Summer 1757
d. Sept. 1784 | *m.*
1777 | Frances
b.unknown
d. late 1778 | Catherine
b. Summer 1765
d. Mar. 20, 1784 | *m. April*
1783 | Edgar
b. 1762
d. Sept.
1801 | Heathcliffe
b. 1764
d. May 1802 | *m. Jan.*
1784 | Isabella
b late 1765
d. June 1797 |

| Hareton *m. Jan. 1, 1803,*
b. June 1778 | = | Catherine *m. Aug. 1801,*
b. Mar. 20 1784 | = | Linton *b. Sept. 1784*
d. Oct. 1801 |

What is *Wuthering Heights* about?

One of the ways in which *Wuthering Heights* is unforgettable is in its quite extraordinary sense of place, and of the bleak, hauntingly alien and austere beauty of the Yorkshire moors. The sense of place is no less remarkable in many of Thomas Hardy's novels, notably *The Return of the Native*, which begins with a long and awesome description

SOCIETY AND THE NOVEL

Jane Austen's "un-interest in the great world, often commented on, is as nothing to Emily Brontë's", says Michael Black. "You are perfectly aware with Jane Austen that you are in the Bath, Hampshire, or London she knew, at the time she knew it." It is a social world she describes, like Flaubert's Normandy, Dickens's London or Tolstoy's St Petersburg. The people of *Wuthering*

Heights and Thrushcross Grange are not like this at all: they "belong to the human race and all time"; the moors represent something primeval and eternal.

Yet *Wuthering Heights* is also, up to a point, a historical novel. In it Emily Brontë was imagining and reconstructing the world in which her parents had grown up – a world already largely lost. In this respect *Wuthering Heights* – the great "Romantic novel" – could profitably be compared with George Eliot's *Middlemarch*. Like *Middlemarch*, published in the early 1870s but set four

of Egdon Heath. After that the Heath is felt as a constant, dread presence that blights or crushes the lives of those who have to live there. So Hardy's doomed Clym Yeobright is described as "permeated with the heath's scenes, with its substance, with its odours":

He might be said to be its product... with its appearance all the first images of his memory were mingled; his estimate of life had been

decades earlier in the period of the 1832 Reform Bill, *Wuthering Heights* is about "provincial" life that spans the three decades from 1771 to 1802. Of course it isn't a "panoramic" novel like *Middlemarch.* There aren't many characters, and its action all takes place within an area of about 16 square miles. But it shows, like *Middlemarch,* what it was like to *live through* a period of immense social change. Brontë was writing, like George Eliot, as an extraordinarily intelligent social historian.

Unlike Eliot, she concentrates in a narrow, very intense way on the changes that took place in a remote area in the West Riding of Yorkshire, and above all in that area's two main houses – the ancient Wuthering Heights, built in 1500 when the ancient Earnshaws were the leading family, and the new or modern Thrushcross Grange where the Lintons live. This contrast between "Ancient" and "Modern" (or, as Q. D. Leavis puts it, between "two cultures") shows why – in Emily Brontë's view, like Jane Austen's when she contemplates modern "improvements" in *Mansfield Park* – Evolution shouldn't be confused with Progress ▪

coloured by it.

His wife Eustacia hates the Heath as a "cruel taskmaster", and when Clym is driven to become a furze-cutter he becomes "a mere parasite of the heath, fretting its source in his daily labour as a moth frets a garment".

Wuthering Heights establishes an unforgettable sense of place just as vividly, but it does so in a very different way: there are no extended natural

FOOD AND FIRE

Food and fire are mentioned often in *Wuthering Heights*. As the critic David Daiches reminds us, what drives Lockwood to the Heights on a cold January day is the fact that the fire in his room at the Grange is out.

> ...*stepping into the room, I saw a servant girl on her knees, surrounded by brushes and coal-scuttles, and raising an infernal dust as she extinguished the flames with heaps of cinders. (2)*

At the Heights, by contrast, Lockwood finds "the radiance of an immense fire". And even after his terrifying dream he comes down in the morning to find Zillah "urging flakes of flame up the chimney with a colossal bellows".

To take another instance, when Isabella arrives at the Heights at Mrs Heathcliff, she finds Joseph bending over the fire making porridge. Though she finds the house looking neglected she notes that still "there was a great fire". The

descriptions. Instead there is an accumulation of brief but intensely rendered details, like the haunting description of the stunted firs and gaunt thorns that immediately follows Lockwood's explanation of what "wuthering" means:

> *Wuthering Heights is the name of Mr. Heathcliff's dwelling. 'Wuthering' being a significant provincial adjective, descriptive of the atmospheric tumult to which its station is*

difference between Linton and the other inhabitants of the Heights is shown to us in one way through difference of diet. He cannot eat the porridge provided and has to eat "boiled milk or tea". When young Catherine finds herself imprisoned at the Heights so that she can marry Linton, Hareton brings her something to eat on a tray.

"All this concrete detail in the novel helps to steady it," says David Daiches. The sense of domestic routine is very strong throughout. But there is a symbolic quality, too, about many of the domestic details.

Clearly, the difference between the deliberately smothered fire at Thrushcross Grange and the roaring fire at Wuthering Heights, or between the diet of Hareton and of Edgar, is part of the total pattern of meaning achieved by the novel. Clearly, too, the sense of people *living well* at Wuthering Heights – Ellen baking the Christmas cake in Chapter 7, "making the house and kitchen cheerful with great fires", to take only one example – has something to do with the novel's emotional centre. In fact, throughout the novel the homely and the familiar and the wild and extravagant go together ∎

exposed in stormy weather. Pure, bracing ventilation they must have up there at all times, indeed: one may guess the power of the north wind blowing over the edge, by the excessive slant of a few stunted firs at the end of the house; and by a range of gaunt thorns all stretching their limbs one way, as if craving alms of the sun. (1)*

That image of the stunted firs with their "excessive slant" is central to the novel – and crucial to understanding it – and it is chillingly recalled after Hindley's funeral in Chapter 17, when Heathcliff lifts the young, defenceless Hareton "on to the table" and mutters "with peculiar gusto":

"Now, my bonny lad, you are mine! And we'll see if one tree won't grow as crooked as another, with the same wind to twist it!" (17)

Wuthering Heights is traditionally seen as being about the timeless romance between Heathcliff and Catherine. This is the version made famous by Hollywood in the greatest film version of the novel, released in 1939 and starring Laurence Olivier. But is Emily Brontë's story really a timeless romance? If so, why are there two Catherines in the book, while there is only one in the film? Indeed the film finishes just a few

*Throughout this book, the numbers in brackets refer to the chapters from which quotations are taken.

minutes after the first Catherine dies, eliminating not just the second Catherine and her romance with Hareton Earnshaw but the whole of the second generation. Many of the novel's critics, like Hollywood, concentrate on the first half of the novel, but this leaves unanswered the question of what the second half is about: what it's doing and why it's there.

The second problem with the traditional view of *Wuthering Heights* is the nature of the relationship between Heathcliff and the first Catherine. The novel takes a much less romantic view of this than the film. As Q.D. Leavis argued in a revolutionary essay in 1969 – an essay which in its "mature authority" dwarfs other critical essays on the novel, in Frank Kermode's view – Catherine never thinks of Heathcliff as a potential husband or mate. On his side there is an unrequited sexual passion, on hers the profound love of a sister for a brother. In Leavis's view, and I believe she's right, the critics who think otherwise have simply failed to read the novel attentively, so that their accounts of it would make more sense if they were writing instead about the 1939 film.

Brontë is very much concerned with deep emotion in *Wuthering Heights*, but not in any straightforward romantic sense. This is a novel in which the characters are driven by forces and passions they don't understand and over which they have no control. As the description of the "stunted firs" with their "excessive slant" suggests, it is a novel much preoccupied with growing up – which means, for the most part, growing up crooked. Its characters are victims, like Hardy's characters in *The Return of the Native*, of the unforgiving environment into which they are born.

If we are reading the novel attentively, the age of the characters is very important. Catherine is not even in her teens when she meets her future husband, and is only 19 when she dies after giving birth. She is only 12 when her father dies and her brother launches his brutal reign of terror; Heathcliff is about 13. And they are even younger, of course, in the opening chapters of the novel.

We have only a glimpse of Earnshaw's legitimate children, Catherine and Hindley, before he departs for Liverpool, but the glimpse seems all the more telling because it follows a pattern that is, as Q.D. Leavis has observed, familiar in folk tales like *Beauty and the Beast*, where the departing merchant father asks his children what presents they would like him to bring back, and returns with the Beast. When old Earnshaw asks his "bonny man", as he calls Hindley, what he would like, young Hindley wants a violin. He is apparently a sensitive child, and there is an obvious, almost formulaic contrast with his much younger and already wilful sister who wants a "whip", or riding

Opposite: poster for the 1939 film of Wuthering Heights. *The film depicts only 16 of the book's 34 chapters, eliminating the second generation of characters.*

am torn with *Desire* tortured by hate!

SAMUEL GOLDWYN

presents

WUTHERING HEIGHTS

co-starring

ERLE OBERON · LAURENCE OLIVIER · DAVID NIVEN

FLORA ROBSON · DONALD CRISP · GERALDINE FITZGERALD · *Released thru* UNITED ARTISTS

Directed by WILLIAM WYLER

crop. Nothing that we see of Hindley after this suggests that music has any part in his miserable life, but that is because whatever life young Hindley might have had dies when his father returns from Liverpool and transfers his affections to the new arrival. Hindley is no longer his father's "bonny man", and this withdrawal of love warps and twists Hindley like one of the stunted firs – just as Hindley's hatred of Heathcliff will quickly warp and twist him too, and Heathcliff will try to warp and twist the second generation. This is a story of revenge as much as it is a story of love.

Almost a hundred years after *Wuthering Heights* was first published, Joyce Cary's painfully moving though now largely forgotten novel

DIALECT IN *WUTHERING HEIGHTS*

Some writers, notably Dickens, use what linguists call "eye-dialect", for instance by writing "wos" for "was". This device doesn't represent any different sound or pronunciation. Rather, illiterate spelling is being used to give the impression of dialect, to remind us that the character is, say, a Cockney.

Brontë's decision to reproduce Joseph's dialect so faithfully, through a complicated orthography, was very unusual, and original. It was also one of the many things in her novel that alarmed her sister Charlotte, who feared that this recording of Joseph's dialect would be "incomprehensible" to the "Southern reader".∎

Charley is my Darling (1940) traced the process that turned a sensitive child into a juvenile delinquent and then into a criminal. Cary's point, reinforced in his preface to the novel, is that children need help before they can begin to understand moral problems and make moral judgements. Cary's preface could also apply to Brontë's novel, and echoes a remark made by G.H. Lewes about the characters in *Wuthering Heights* when he reviewed it on first publication:

> "such brutes we should all be, or the most of us, were our lives as insubordinate to the law; were our affections and sympathies as little cultivated, our imaginations as undirected".*

I think Brontë would have applauded Lewes's point, which underlies so much that she set out to do when she was revising and greatly extending her earlier, rejected version of *Wuthering Heights*. The high level of violence in the novel, Pauline Nestor argues in her introduction to the latest Penguin edition, challenges our assumptions "about the restraining limits of civilised behaviour". So too does Lockwood's narrative – his conventional perspective frames the story, but because he is so conventional he chronically misreads the situation.

*G. H. Lewes was the novelist George Eliot's wonderfully intelligent companion for many years in which the pair bravely defied Victorian conventions by "living in sin".

Michael Black makes a similar point in *The Literature of Fidelity*. Writing Heathcliff off as demonic, or turning him into a "goblin" or a "werewolf" is a mere device – a way in which "ordinariness holds off its sense of failure; failure in this case to reach a lonely, suffering and violent man". *Wuthering Heights,* says Black, is "a deeply subversive novel", whose overall effect "is to go on disturbing the reader". It rebukes our hard-headedness, our conventionality, suggesting that an "inability to feel things deeply" is a sign of "smallness, not wisdom". In this sense it is a timeless book, worlds apart from the social novels of Jane Austen's Bath or Dickens's London. The Heights are intensely seen and felt as a place; but the house is already three hundred years old when the action unfurls in 1801; it represents something ancestral, and the moors represent something primeval and eternal. Equally, the chief characters don't belong to 1770 and Yorkshire so much as the human race and all time. By the end of the book things have taken place between heroic characters which the surviving inhabitants, smaller people, look back on with dread and doubtful understanding.

Why does Brontë use so many narrators?

Because of the unusual way in which it is told, *Wuthering Heights* has been compared to a Chinese box puzzle. It starts with the date "1801", when Lockwood begins writing his journal after his first meeting with Heathcliff. Lockwood is the primary narrator, who records all the information he receives from Ellen Dean or "Nelly", the novel's main narrator. Her story is then inside his. As in Anne Brontë's novel, *The Tenant of Wildfell Hall*, a woman's narrative is framed by a man's.

But Nelly's story includes the sometimes lengthy stories she has heard from other characters, and it is remarkable and, on the face of it absurdly unrealistic, that all these characters can remember and transmit not only other people's speeches but their intonation. Remember – which is easy, because it's unforgettable – Heathcliff's outcry when he wrenches open the attic of the window that Lockwood has broken, "bursting, as he pulled at it, into an uncontrollable passion of tears":

> *"Come in! come in!" he sobbed. "Cathy, do come. Oh, do – once more! Oh! my heart's darling, hear me this time – Catherine, at last!" (3)*

We recall this hundreds of pages later, when

Heathcliff's corpse is discovered under the same lattice window. The speech's distinctive punctuation and emphases – the dashes and exclamation marks, and the two perfectly placed, heartrending emphases on "*once*" and "*this*" – help to make this outcry so memorable. Heathcliff constantly uses dashes and exclamation marks, and is not much given to the colons and semi-colons that characters like the educated Edgar and Lockwood and even the self-educated Nelly constantly use. Of course we never choose between dashes or semicolons when we *speak*, only when we write.

But if what might be called this perfect relay system of multiple narratives is in a sense absurd, in another it is astonishingly effective. To dismiss Brontë's method as unrealistic is like objecting that great novels like George Eliot's *Middlemarch* and Tolstoy's *War and Peace* are unrealistic because they depend on omniscient narrators who know everything about the characters. In real life there are no omniscient narrators who can cruise at will through different people's skulls, explaining what they have not yet understood or thought through.

Brontë's method of narration is closer to the confused way we learn things in real life. Heathcliff is the central character of *Wuthering Heights* but there is no way in which he could tell his own story, and he has no interest in what other characters (except Cathy) think about him. Using multiple narrators enabled Brontë to explore the ways in which different characters react to Heathcliff, and it is striking that we often feel most sympathy for him when others are regarding him as a monster or as beyond their comprehension. The way Brontë uses her multiple narrators also heightens the effect of the story because of the contrast between the manic emotions being described and the matter-of-fact way they are reported. "It is to what might be called the sublime deadpan of the telling that the extraordinary force of the novel can largely be attributed," says David Daiches. The chain of narrators "serve to mediate between the barbarism of the story and the civility of the reader," says Frank Kermode.

So we never go inside Heathcliff in the way, for example, we go inside Tolstoy's Prince Andrew after he has fallen for Natasha in *War and Peace*:

Having lit the candle he sat up in bed, then got up, then lay down again not at all troubled by sleeplessness: his soul was as fresh and joyful as if he had stepped out of a stuffy room into God's own fresh air. It did not enter his head that he was in love with Natasha, he was not thinking about her, but only picturing her to himself, and in consequence all life appeared in a new light.

There is nothing like this wonderful chapter in

Brontë's novel. Her mode of narration doesn't encourage us to see her characters in this way. Thus in *Wuthering Heights*, we can never be sure whether or not Heathcliff kills Hindley or allows him to choke to death – he was "snorting like a horse", we are told, after sending Joseph off to fetch the doctor. When Nelly hears of the death of her "old master and foster-brother" she rushes to the Heights, wondering: "Had he had fair play?"

Scenes like this have an uncertainty which is all too familiar in life, but could not be sustained if the story were being told by an omniscient narrator. In *Wuthering Heights* we are often unsure how to react, or how to judge the people we are reading about. Our uncertainty is heightened by the fact that while the multiple narrators may all be reliable as transmitters of information they are by no means reliable judges of what is going on.

Can we trust Lockwood?

Lockwood and Nelly are not unreliable narrators, like the governess in Henry James's *The Turn of the Screw* or the narrator in Ford Madox Ford's *The Good Soldier*. We can trust their apparently verbatim reports of what happened many years before. A few modern critics, notably the American J. Hillis Miller, have taken a hard deconstructionist line – believing we should be sceptical about what they tell us – but most critics and readers assume that, unless there are clear signals to the contrary, whatever Lockwood reports that Nelly said that Heathcliff or Joseph said is just what they *did* say. Still, even as the novel encourages us to make this assumption, it repeatedly shows that we also need to make an important distinction between reliable narrators and unreliable judges.

The novel's opening pages show how Lockwood – like Jonathan Swift's Gulliver – is an exceptionally keen observer of things but a very poor judge of people and situations. He continually notices and describes things that Nelly, an insider who has spent all of her adult life in the Heights or the Grange, would either not notice or would not think to describe. When Lockwood first sees Heathcliff he even notices what his host's fingers are doing:

> *A capital fellow! He little imagined how my heart warmed towards him when I beheld his black eyes withdraw so suspiciously under their brows, as I rode up, and when his fingers sheltered themselves, with a jealous resolution, still further in his waistcoat, as I announced my name. (1)*

Clearly, Heathcliff does not want to shake hands: his fingers are already in his waistcoat when Lockwood announces his name, and then shelter themselves "still further" with a "jealous resolution". His description is witty in a rather effete, self-regarding way, but in this case his habitual self-regard and self-absorption blinds him to what is almost immediately apparent to the reader: Lockwood, who affects to be a misanthrope, cannot recognise the real thing when he meets it.

His conceit, condescension and self-regard are all the more obviously disabling when his initially instructive, objective description of Heathcliff quickly slides back to Me, Me, Me.

He is a dark-skinned gypsy in aspect, in dress

BOUNDARIES IN *WUTHERING HEIGHTS*

Wuthering Heights, as plenty of critics have noted, is full of physical boundaries like walls, windows, gates, doorways and locks. These boundaries, as Pauline Nestor says, "are frequently guarded and just as frequently breached". They can suggest psychic as well as physical barriers, says Dorothy Van Ghent, who sees Lockwood's name as suggesting his ability to "shut out the powers of darkness" and the window-pane on which the child scratches as "the medium, treacherously transparent, separating the 'inside' from the 'outside', the 'human' from the alien and terrible 'other'". This windowpane imagery is important, too,

and manners a gentleman: that is, as much a gentleman as many a country squire: rather slovenly, perhaps, yet not looking amiss with his negligence... Possibly, some people might suspect him of a degree of underbred pride; I have a sympathetic chord within that tells me it is nothing of the sort; I know, by instinct, his reserve springs from an aversion to showy displays of feeling – to manifestations of mutual kindness. He'll love and hate equally under cover, and esteem it a species of impertinence to be loved or hated again. No, I'm running on too fast: I bestow my attributes too liberally upon him.

when Heathcliff and Catherine look through the window of the Lintons' drawing room.

Characters in the novel are often trying to keep others out of somewhere or at a distance. What Nestor calls "this struggle to exclude" is at its sharpest in the image of the wall separating the cultivated park of the Grange from the wildness of the moors. "This barrier is, however, constantly breached from both sides as Heathcliff comes and goes at will and the youthful Catherine, despite her father's prohibition, easily devises strategies for escape." The Grange is vulnerable to intruders, however, partly because its occupants want it to be, as Sandra Gilbert and Susan Gubar point out in *The Madwoman in the Attic*. On Catherine's first incursion there she doesn't so much voluntarily enter the house as become seized by it (as she is trying to escape). Similarly, Edgar is

We then learn of Lockwood's non-existent affair with the "fascinating creature" he had met in some fashionable southern "sea-coast" spa but was content to admire from afar:

I was thrown into the company of a most fascinating creature: a real goddess in my eyes, as long as she took no notice of me. I 'never told my love' vocally; still, if looks have language, the merest idiot might have guessed I was over head and ears: she understood me at last, and looked a return – the sweetest of all imaginable looks.

The finely calibrated comedy that follows when

irresistibly drawn to the Heights despite witnessing Catherine's temper and being warned off by Nelly: "Take warning, and begone!" He can't: "he possessed the power to depart, as much as a cat possesses the power to leave a mouse half killed, or a bird half eaten" (8).

"*Wuthering Heights* is a novel preoccupied with the idea of boundary," says the American critic John Matthews. It "haunts the sites of division – between self and other, individual and family, nature and culture, mortality and immortality". Heathcliff himself, as the distinguished critic Frank Kermode has argued, seems posed half way between savagery and civilisation.

"He is often introduced as if characteristically standing outside, or entering, or leaving, a door... His origins are equally betwixt and between: the gutter or the royal origin imagined for him by Nelly; prince

Lockwood enters the Heights and makes one mistake after another confirms that this keen observer of things is a hopeless judge of human relationships because he hasn't had any, unless with "mamma". But then, in a clever, somewhat mischievous way the novel sets up a kind of false trail involving Lockwood and the second Catherine.

As we have seen, Lockwood's first function is to be the wholly reliable recorder of what Nelly says other characters said and did. His second function is to mediate, like Sir Walter Scott's Waverley, between North and South when he confronts an unfamiliar, harsh and violent world. Even his

or pauper, American or Lascar, child of God or devil. This betweenness persists, I think: Heathcliff, for instance, fluctuates between poverty and riches; also between virility and impotence. To Catherine he is between brother and lover; he slept with her as a child, and again in death, but not between latency and extinction. He has much force, yet fathers an exceptionally puny child. Domestic yet savage like the dogs, bleak yet full of fire like the house, he bestrides the great opposites: love and death (the necrophiliac confession), culture and nature ('half-civilised ferocity') in a posture that cannot be explained by a generic formula ('Byronic' or 'Gothic').

"He stands also between a past and a future; when his force expires the old Earnshaw family moves into the future associated with the civilised Grange" ▪

mistakes can then be instructive for the reader, involving as they do southern misconceptions. But there is then the question about what Lockwood himself can learn by extracting (as he puts it) "wholesome medicines from Mrs Dean's bitter herbs", and even by wooing the second Catherine. Lockwood considers this last possibility at the end of Part One, while fearing that the daughter might turn out to be "a second edition of the mother!" But this turns out to be a comically false trail, as we might guess when Lockwood is babbling in his silly, emotionally retarded way about the need to "beware of the fascination that lurks in Catherine Heathcliff's brilliant eyes".

Still, Lockwood's eye for things is so keen that even as he enters the Heights he notices the date "1500" and the name "Hareton Earnshaw" above the "principal door" and "among" the "grotesque carvings" of "a wilderness of crumbling griffins and shameless little boys". He is immediately and characteristically curious, but wryly records in his journal that it seemed better not to bother Heathcliff with questions: "his attitude at the door appeared to demand my speedy entrance, or complete departure".

What he sees when he goes inside is meticulously described:

One step brought us into the family sitting-

room, without any introductory lobby or passage: they call it here "the house" preeminently. It includes kitchen and parlour, generally, but I believe at Wuthering Heights the kitchen is forced to retreat altogether into another quarter; at least I distinguished a chatter of tongues, and a clatter of culinary utensils deep within; and I observed no signs of roasting, boiling, or baking about the huge fireplace; nor any glitter of copper saucepans and tin cullenders of the walls. (1)

This is the first of many such richly specific descriptions that establish the crucial contrasts between the Heights and the Grange and the different potentialities for life they represent. In many cases the changes that we see taking place in the Heights, in the last decades of the 18th century, had taken place in southern England more than a century earlier.

So, for example, 17th-century architecture shows how – as the family rather than the "household" became the social unit with a correspondingly new emphasis on privacy – the hall became a more or less imposing vestibule leading to separate family rooms, which were carefully segregated from the servants' quarters. In Thrushcross Grange that segregation is taken for granted, along with costly family amenities like plush carpets and chandeliers. The Grange clearly has many servants who can be called or fetched, for example when Heathcliff is to be ejected; but they are rarely seen and we don't know how many there are; as in Jane Austen's novels the house is "empty" when the family is away, although there are servants inside. But Lockwood's description shows how in Wuthering Heights "one step" took him into the large living area that was called the "house". There is no separate "parlour" that is used exclusively by the family.

Later, we learn how, when old Earnshaw was the "master" and Nelly and Joseph had finished their tasks, they would both sit in this large and warm "apartment" with the family. We then learn how this traditional way of life was changed when Earnshaw dies in 1777 and Hindley, Nelly's new "master", returns from the south, after acquiring his college degree, his southern bride, and some distinctly southern preferences and expectations. But of course Lockwood only arrives at the Grange in 1801; in tracing all such past history the indispensable informant is Nelly Dean – another reliable narrator who is also an unreliable judge.

Is Nelly Dean also a bad judge?

Nelly, who tells most of the story, could hardly be more unlike Lockwood as a character. We frequently see her engaged in household activities like baking a Christmas cake, but since she has spent nearly all of her life working in the Heights or at the Grange it would never occur to her to describe the gleamingly clean kitchen where she bakes the cake, or to describe the house.

On the other hand it is Nelly, who is so much less concerned with things than with people, who explains how a parlour was nearly constructed in 1777. As she recalls, when old Earnshaw was master of the Heights and when she and Joseph had finished their tasks, they would both sit in this large, warm "apartment" together with the family proper, but when old Earnshaw dies and Hindley returns from the south with his bride, this immediately changes.

> ...on the very day of his return, he told Joseph and me we must thenceforth quarter ourselves in the back-kitchen and leave the house for him. Indeed he would have carpeted and papered a small spare room for a parlour; but his wife expressed such pleasure at the white floor, and huge glowing fire-place, at the pewter dishes and delft-case, and the wide space there was to move about in, where they usually sat, that he thought it unnecessary to her comfort, and so dropped the intention. (6)

The pleasure that the unpretentious Frances takes

in this "abode or style of living" tells in her favour, while also suggesting that her own background has been more deprived – one likely reason why Hindley did not tell his father of his marriage. Yet poor Frances's appreciation of the warmth and intimacy of life at the Heights is still largely aesthetic. In fact, this "style of living" has been shaped by harsh exigencies – as we realise when Isabella comes to live at the Heights and is appalled by the lack of a parlour and privacy. Coming from the superflous luxuries of life at the Grange, she can take no pleasure in the dogs "under the dresser", or in the "gaudily painted canisters" that have been placed "along the ledge... by way of ornament".

Although a born mother whom we see caring for each of the Heights children in turn, the uncomplaining Nelly has no man, no family, little money, and no more security than her ill-defined "place" affords. We learn that she was born in 1757, two months after Hindley; she first came to the Heights as a child when her old but vigorously healthy mother was engaged as Catherine's nurse, and became Hindley's "early playmate". That Nelly inherits her mother's remarkable constitution is important because her own sometimes questionable judgments are those of somebody who is naturally "healthy" and "normal" in a novel which is constantly questioning what it means to be normal.

The first Catherine makes this point in Chapter 15 when she says that Nelly thinks herself "better" because she has "full health and strength". Earlier, she has railed against Nelly in similar vein:

> *"To hear you, people might think you were the mistress!" she cried. "You want setting down in your right place!" (11)*

This is another point where we see the novel's grasp of social history. Nelly, whom Edgar always calls "Ellen", must put up with such wounding treatment from the houshold's First Lady because her own "right place" in it is so painfully uncertain: she is not quite a servant, but nor is she a member of the family.

After her mother's death, the teenage Nelly's natural capacities ensure that she is soon managing the household and looking after each of its children in turn. When Edgar and Catherine marry they urge Nelly to move from the Heights to the Grange and promise more "munificent" wages, but her immediate reason for refusing is that "little Hareton" is "nearly five": "I had just begun to teach him his letters." Unlike Lockwood, she naturally and constantly cares for others. The characterisation of Nelly through the four decades in question is one of the novel's triumphs, although the triumph, as Q.D. Leavis observes, is |so quietly achieved.

One of the most successful indications of the passage of time is Nelly Dean's change, from the quick-moving and quick-witted girl who for little Hareton's sake copes with the drunken murderous Hindley, to the stout, breathless, middle-aged woman who, though still spirited, cannot save [young] Cathy from a forced marriage.

In short, there are good reasons for agreeing with Charlotte Brontë's wholly admiring view of Nelly in her 1850 Preface. "For a specimen of true benevolence and homely fidelity, look at the character of Nelly Dean..."

But there are also good reasons for *disagreeing* with it, as Mrs Humphry Ward pointed out in a strong rebuttal of Charlotte's Preface in 1900. Dissenting firmly from Charlotte's eulogy, Mrs Ward emphasises the repeated ways in which Nelly disobeys her three successive masters' instructions and even betrays their trust.

In the first instance, Nelly disobeys Mr Earnshaw when he returns from Liverpool with the foundling, and tells Nelly to put him to bed with the other children: instead, Nelly puts "it on the landing of the stairs, hoping that it might be gone on the morrow". Nelly's disobedience here is very clear, and the older, narrating Nelly, looking back on it, condemns her own

"cowardice and inhumanity".

Nelly's disobedience when Hindley becomes her new master is less likely to prompt disapproval, and seems more like a vindication of what Charlotte Brontë and Leavis see as Nelly's essentially "feminine" and "motherly" nature: when Hindley insists that Heathcliff be confined in his room without food, she smuggles the poor lad down to the kitchen to feed him.

But if this disobedience is defensible, Nelly's behaviour to Edgar Linton is much less so. Mary Ward is shocked by what she calls Nelly's "treacherous, cruel, and indefensible" betrayal of Linton's wishes and interests, despite claiming that this is the "master" she (Nelly) most admires. "She becomes the go-between for Catherine and Heathcliff," writes Mary Ward, and she

> knowingly allows her charge Catherine, on the eve of her confinement, to fast in solitude and delirium for three days and nights, without saying a word to Edgar Linton, Catherine's affectionate husband, and her master, who was in the house all the time. It is her breach of trust which brings about Catherine's dying scene with Heathcliff, just as it is her disobedience and unfaith which really betray Catherine's child into the hands of her enemies.

To these grave charges might be added another, which is that Nelly does not want Catherine to know that she fetched Edgar in Chapter 11, when she was frightened by the quarrel between Catherine and Heathcliff. This, and the anxious Edgar's arrival, precipitates the terrible, climactic scene when Catherine throws the keys into the fire; but Nelly wants Catherine to go on believing that Edgar was "listening at the door", not that she herself had gone to fetch him. In Chapter 12 the dying Catherine explodes with rage when she discovers that "Nelly has played traitor": "Nelly is my hidden enemy. You witch!"

Well-meaning and "normal" as she is, Nelly's judgement is at best erratic and sometimes disastrous. It helps to cause the tragedy which she so convincingly describes.

Is old Earnshaw Heathcliff's father?

Near the beginning of Q.D. Leavis's 1969 essay "A Fresh Approach to *Wuthering Heights*", we find this startling sentence:

> Clearly, Heathcliff was originally the illegitimate son and Catherine's half-brother, which would explain why, though so attached to him by early associations and natural sympathies, Catherine never really thinks of him as a possible lover either before or after marriage.

We know that Emily Brontë sent an early, shorter but presumably complete version of her novel to the publisher Henry Culter, and that when he rejected it she revised and greatly extended the earlier version. Leavis argues that in this "immature draft" Heathcliff was Earnshaw's "illegitimate son and Catherine's half-brother", and that the "favourite Romantic theme of incest therefore must have been the impulse behind the earliest conception of *Wuthering Heights*". Nonetheless, she argues, this sensationally Byronic* "incest theme" was carefully "written out" when the "mature" Brontë set to work revising her novel in the summer of 1846.

Leavis's first argument is important, though we should be wary of words like "clearly" and phrases like "therefore must have been". Leavis's second argument, which she presents as following from the first, is that when the "mature" Brontë decided to remove the sensational "incest theme" she had a major problem:

> Rejecting this story for a more mature intention, Emily Brontë was left with hopeless inconsistencies on her hands, for while Catherine's

*The Brontë sisters were all fascinated by the great Romantic poet Byron, and the darkly thrilling "Romantic theme of incest" became as important in his life as well as his poetry, through his relationship with his half-sister Augusta Leigh. When Byron left England for Europe he was widely thought to have fathered Augusta's child Medora, although Augusta's husband regarded the child as his own.

feelings about Heathcliff are never sexual (though she feels the bond of sympathy with a brother to be more important to her than her feelings for Edgar), Heathcliff's feelings for her are always those of a lover. As Heathcliff has been written out as a half-brother, Catherine's innocent refusal to see that there is anything in her relation to him incompatible with her position as a wife, becomes preposterous...

The example Leavis leans on most heavily in her argument that *Wuthering Heights* began as a novel about incest is the way it begins. This, she says, "suggests that we are going to have a regional version of the sub-plot of *Lear*":

The troubles of the Earnshaws started when the father brought home the boy Heathcliff (of which he gives an unconvincing explanation and for whom he shows an unaccountable weakness) and forced him on the protesting family; Heathcliff "the cuckoo" by intrigue soon ousts the legitimate son Hindley and, like Edmund, Gloucester's natural son in *Lear*, his malice brings about the ruin of two families (the Earnshaws and the Lintons, his rival getting the name Edgar by attraction from Lear).

Perhaps the most interesting part of this argument is Leavis's passing observation about Earnshaw's explanation for bringing home Heathcliff. This, she says, is "unconvincing", and she is right.

We never learn why Mr Earnshaw had to go to Liverpool, or why he decided to walk all the way there and back – "sixty miles each way" – when there were horses in the stables, and when, as he says, his "money and time" were "both limited". Since Nelly mentions that it "was the beginning of harvest", we might wonder whether the horses were needed on the farm – but wouldn't the master have been needed too? Whatever unexplained business he had in Liverpool doesn't take him long, nor can he have spent long trying to discover the "starving and homeless" child's "owner". He still arrives home just three days later, as he said he

CHARLOTTE BRONTË'S 1850 PREFACE

Charlotte's 1850 Preface provided the foundation for the Brontë legend that Lucasta Miller so ably dissects in *The Brontë Myth* (2001). As Miller notes, Charlotte turned Emily into "an unthinking sibyl", and never considered her sister as a well read, highly conscious artist.

What "broods" over the novel, Charlotte argued, is "a horror of great darkness". It is no wonder she seized on Nelly as "a specimen of true benevolence and homely fidelity". She was anxious to "point to those spots where clouded daylight and the eclipsed sun still attest their existence". Nelly, to Charlotte, is a kind of compensation, a reassuring sign that Emily was not altogether cut off from normative and healthy

would, while carrying the children's presents and the child, too, for much of the 60-mile walk. When he throws himself "into a chair, laughing and groaning", and says he "would not have such another walk for the three kingdoms", we might wonder whether he ever went to Liverpool.

The furious Mrs Earnshaw is clearly not satisfied by her husband's explanation of how he came by the "gipsy brat", and Nelly recalls how "frightened" she was when Earnshaw unbundled his greatcoat and the child tumbled out. Years later, when she repeats Earnshaw's "tale" to Lockwood she excuses its shortcomings by saying that the "master" was "half dead with fatigue" and

emotions, despite having created the first Catherine, with her "perverse passion and passionate perversity", and, even worse, the brutal Hindley and the monstrous Heathcliff, who "stands unredeemed, never once swerving in his arrow-straight course to perdition". Having formed these beings, Charlotte wrote, her sister "did not know what she had done... Whether it is right or advisable to create beings like Heathcliff, I do not know: I scarcely think it is."

Charlotte's "Official Version" wasn't challenged until 50 years later, when Mrs Humphry Ward published her 1900 Preface to the Haworth edition. Mary Augusta Ward – a grand-daughter of Thomas Arnold of Rugby and niece of his son Matthew Arnold – was herself a notable novelist and a founder of the Woman's Anti-Suffrage League. Her own Preface emphasises Emily's artistry and wide reading. She also disagreed with Charlotte's judgment of characters, most notably Heathcliff but also Nelly ∎

that she couldn't "make out" all he said since his "scolding" wife was making such a noise.

Why pick up this particular "starving, and houseless" child, which Earnshaw maintains was a complete stranger he saw in the street? At this time and for long afterwards the streets of Liverpool were full of destitute Irish refugees, fleeing from a country constantly devastated by famine and the English. But Nelly also tells Lockwood that the new arrival could "walk and talk", and babbled away in "some gibberish that nobody could understand".

Terry Eagleton and other critics have suggested that the "dirty" child is Irish and speaking in Erse. Yet the novel floats another possibility when Heathcliff is repeatedly described as looking like a gypsy – "a dark-skinned gipsy in aspect," as Lockwood describes him in the opening pages (in which case he would have been babbling in Romany, not Erse). But where is the gypsy mother? One possible mother is mentioned in Chapter Six after Heathcliff and Catherine are captured in the Grange. When the "cowardly" Linton children "crept nearer" to examine the "frightful thing" called Heathcliff, the "lisping" Isabella declares that he is "exactly like the son of the fortune-teller, that stole my tame pheasant". Is Brontë hinting at Heathcliff's origins? Why did she include the startling detail about a gypsy fortune-

teller, unless she wanted the reader to register it? And why allow Earnshaw only three, not four or five days in which to accomplish his mysterious 120-mile walk?

In other 19th-century novels the discrepancies and omissions in Earnshaw's "tale" that make us wonder whether he ever went to Liverpool would prepare the way for some later revelation, like the revelation about Mrs Rochester in *Jane Eyre* – some unforgiven past affair with a gypsy fortune-teller, perhaps, or some other shameful skeleton in the Earnshaw family cupboard involving a reprobate brother, or a tragically "fallen" sister.

But what, more than anything else, might have prompted any of the characters in the novel who speculate on Heathcliff's mysterious origins to wonder whether he might be Earnshaw's natural son is the astonishingly rapid and cruel way in which – within the few days when Catherine and Heathcliff first grow "very thick" – Earnshaw transfers all of his love and affection to the cuckoo-child he has brought into the family nest. It is this, not the mere arrival of the foster-child, that has a devastating effect on the Earnshaw family.

Nelly is being a reliable narrator but a poor judge when she tells Lockwood that "from the beginning" Heathcliff "bred bad feeling in the house". Heathcliff can hardly be blamed for being brought to Wuthering Heights, and as Nelly herself has just recalled, he is very cruelly treated after his arrival:

> *He seemed a sullen, patient child, hardened,*
> *perhaps, to ill-treatment: he would stand*
> *Hindley's blows without winking or shedding a*
> *tear, and my pinches moved him only to draw in a*
> *breath, and open his eyes as if he had hurt*
> *himself by accident, and nobody was to blame.*
>
> > *This endurance made old Earnshaw furious*
> *when he discovered his son persecuting the poor,*
> *fatherless child, as he called him. He took to*
> *Heathcliff strangely, believing all he said (for*
> *that matter, he said precious little, and generally*
> *the truth) and petting him up above Cathy, who*
> *was too mischievous and wayward to be a*
> *favourite. (4)*

Leavis believes that while the rapid and cruel change in Earnshaw made sense in Brontë's original manuscript it didn't in the published novel when the incest theme was "written out" and Brontë was left with "hopeless inconsistencies on her hands". Why would old Earnshaw become so fond of Heathcliff if he *wasn't* his illegitimate son? Her argument is interesting but unprovable. No trace remains of the original, rejected novel. The only evidence there is to support Leavis's argument is in the final, revised version, since that is all we have. And it leaves us in the dark.

But what of Leavis's second and much more

important argument, that Cathy never feels for Heathcliff what he feels for her? Leavis believes that this argument follows from, even depends upon, her argument that Heathcliff was originally Catherine's half-brother. But of course it doesn't. It is perfectly plausible that Cathy comes to feel a sister's love for Heathcliff, even if he is her foster brother not her half-brother – and that she never feels the same way about him as he does about her.

In Chapter 12 the dying, delirious Catherine recalls the trauma she suffered when "I was a child, my father was just buried, and my misery arose from the separation that Hindley had ordered between me and Heathcliff... my all in all, as Heathcliff was at that time". These last words, especially the word "was", show her remembering her husband. But Heathcliff has remained the most important man in her life, just as Maggie Tulliver's brother Tom in George Eliot's *The Mill on the Floss* remains more important to her than any of her suitors, and just as the most important man in Emily Brontë's life was almost certainly her reprobate brother Branwell, who died the year after *Wuthering Heights* was published. But, as Leavis emphasises in her essay, Catherine's feelings for Heathcliff are not like his feelings for her. They are "never sexual": "she feels the bond of sympathy with a brother to be more important to her than her feelings for her young husband". The "love" for Heathcliff that the 15-year-old Catherine tries to explain to Nelly in Chapter Nine "is not love but a need of some fundamental kind that is quite separate from her normal love for Edgar Linton, a love which leads to a happily consummated marriage and the expectation of providing an heir".

This is a tragic situation because "Heathcliff's feelings for her are always those of a lover". Michael Black makes that point more memorably in *The Literature of Fidelity* when he observes that "from first to last" Heathcliff is "clear about his one need: union with Catherine, alive or dead. She wavers, and that causes the tragedy."

Yet this tragic situation is perfectly intelligible and moving if Heathcliff is, as most readers have assumed, Catherine's *foster*-brother and not her half-brother. And it is significant that none of the characters in the novel ever consider the possibility that Earnshaw is Heathcliff's father. It never occurs to Catherine or Nelly. It doesn't occur to Hindley, even though he grows up regarding Heathcliff as the "usurper". We can't know whether it ever occurs to the unforthcoming Heathcliff, but we can be sure that if it did he wouldn't care.

How does Heathcliff's arrival affect the Earnshaw household?

In his classic study, *The Image of Childhood*, Peter Coveney shows how the imaginative preoccupation with childhood as a separate state is distinctively "Romantic", and how Romantic poets like Blake and Wordsworth were profoundly concerned with the contrast between childhood Innocence and adult Experience. This contrast, with its insistence on *separate* states of being and an accompanying, sometimes desperate sense of loss, answered to the ways in which we feel ourselves to be both a part of nature and apart from nature. Childhood became part of a world we have lost: as the 18th-century poet Edward Young ruefully put it, we are born originals and become copies or imitations. Brontë, like her sisters, was fascinated by childhood, the deep emotions which spring from it, the way our lives are shaped by it.

So Q.D. Leavis is right, I think, to emphasise the importance of the idyllic "scampers on the moors" that Catherine longingly recalls when she is dying, and when such scampers would no longer satisfy the adult Heathcliff who wants her as his mate. As Leavis observes, a strong influence on the novel, "very much of the period", is "the Romantic image of childhood", with the childish Heathcliff and

Catherine shown as having been "idyllically and innocently happy together" when "roaming the countryside as hardy, primitive Wordsworthian children, 'half savage and hardy and free'". But if Brontë's novel conveys the innocence of childhood it also shows how it can be warped and even destroyed by a lack of love.

The Earnshaw child who is devastated when old Earnshaw returns from Liverpool and brings the still unnamed cuckoo-child into the family nest is not Catherine but Hindley. As Nelly notes in Chapter Four, her young playmate Hindley's life is poisoned by his sense of Heathcliff as the "usurper":

> *the young master had learned to regard his father as an oppressor rather than a friend, and Heathcliff as a usurper of his parent's affections, and his privileges, and he grew bitter with brooding over his injuries.*

So far as the usurpation of the "parent's affections" is concerned, we should notice how "parent's" is singular, not plural, although his mother is still alive. We never see her displaying affection to her husband or any of the children, nor is there any suggestion that she did so before Heathcliff's arrival. The same point is being signalled, just as indirectly, when Nelly becomes more drawn to Heathcliff: the result of that, as she sadly recalls to

Lockwood, was Hindley lost his "last ally". Although Mrs Earnshaw doesn't die until more than a year later, she is no "ally" for her children; when she does die, there is no suggestion that anyone in the family mourns or misses her.

Old Earnshaw is still alive, of course, but Hindley's brutal treatment of Heathcliff, his "favourite", further alienates him from his son, whom he cruelly describes as "naught". Hindley is indeed alone. He loses his sister when she becomes so "thick" with the child the tormented Hindley keeps beating up. After that, Catherine never shows the slightest trace of affection for her natural brother, and when the 20-year-old Hindley becomes the new "master" of the Heights and launches his reign of terror, Catherine's contempt for her brother turns to hatred.

In Chapter Nine, when she is trying to justify her decision to marry Edgar, she refers to her natural brother with deep and abiding hatred as "that wicked man in there who brought Heathcliff so low" that "it would degrade me to marry Heathcliff, now". In Chapter 10, when Heathcliff returns after his three-year absence and speaks of his intention to kill Hindley, Catherine is not in the least concerned. Hindley has a kind of second chance when he goes off to college in the South and returns with Frances, the wife who loves him and whom he loves nearly as much as he "adored" himself – as Nelly waspishly observes. But when

Frances dies Hindley is thrown back on his own resources, and has none.

Hindley is – to borrow the admirable phrase Michael Black uses to describe Heathcliff – "presented with some care as a humanly conceivable evolution". We see how the boy who asked for a violin, when his father promised to bring his "bonny young man" a present from Liverpool, turns into the brutally violent alcoholic man, who beats and degrades young Heathcliff, is indifferent to his own small son Hareton (who is frightened of him), and is no less indifferent to his young sister's welfare and education. Catherine is only 12 when Hindley becomes the new "master".

Catherine can already read and write, but there are no books other than the gross theological tracts. For the rest of her short life, which is already more than half over, she never reads a book and hates her husband's retreats into the library. In this respect Lockwood is unconsciously inspired when he builds a "pyramid" of books to try to stop the child-ghost entering. Although we never hear of Heathcliff reading either, it is clear that he does read, at least in his later life: he comments in a brutal but incisive way on how Isabella's taste for trashy romantic novelettes has impaired her judgment, and Heathcliff knows enough about 18th century property laws to run rings around Magistrate Edgar Linton JP, whose birth and money are enough to secure these entitlements.

Nelly tells Lockwood that old Earnshaw was always "grave and strict" with his children, and "relentless" about "ruling his children rigidly" (which, rather curiously, never comes through in any of the film or TV adaptations). Since Nelly is growing up too in these early chapters – there is only two months difference between her age and Hindley's – she is shrewd to see how Hindley's mind is poisoned by his sense of Heathcliff as a "usurper".

Why does Cathy marry Edgar Linton?

Nelly is no less shrewd to observe the different dynamic at work in Catherine's more complicated case, whenever her grave and strict father tells her: "I cannot love thee, thou'rt worse than thy brother."

That made her cry, at first; and then, being repulsed continually hardened her, and she laughed if I told her to say she was sorry for her faults, and beg to be forgiven. (5)

The dynamic that shapes young Catherine's development is evident long before her father rejects her in favour of the mysterious foundling. Her wilfulness, which is so inseparable from her "spirit" – that key word in this novel and in so many Romantic novels and poems (Nelly tells Lockwood that "spirit" was what the Lintons lacked) – is the problematic element, not least for Nelly, who has by then also lost her mother and has to make her own way as part of the Earnshaw household without ever being "family".

The older, narrating Nelly recalls how spirited young Catherine was, as the indulged baby of the Earnshaw family, and how enchanting she could be when she was happy and wished to please or share her happiness. But the older Nelly also recalls how Catherine would assert her wishes through pinches or punches – and how she, Nelly, disliked this intensely. Over the years, Nelly's relationship with Catherine becomes the most difficult in her rather thinly populated life, although years have to pass before she firmly concludes: "I did not like her."

In tracing Catherine's arrested emotional development, the novel very impressively shows how it moves through different stages. One of the stages comes when her father withdraws his love, "petting up" his new favourite "far above Cathy". Being "repulsed", we are told, "continually hardened her". Then, when old Earnshaw dies and his warped son launches his reign of terror with the help of the Christian sadist Joseph, Catherine, who is only 12, becomes more unmanageable than ever. She cannot even find paper in the house when she wants to keep a diary, like so many girls of her age, and has to use the margins of a theological tome. After the momentous visit to the Grange, she and Heathcliff are forbidden to be with each other.

Even before they visit the Grange, she has become the centre and circumference of Heathcliff's emotional world; he has covered himself with a steely carapace that only she can penetrate. But when he tells Nelly how he would shatter all of the Grange's great glass panes if Catherine "wished to return" and the Lintons would not "let her out", he is recognising the more threatening possibility that she may *not* wish to return. Returning to Heathcliff also means, for Cathy, returning to the oppression and misery of their life at the Heights. This, of course, is the germ of that guilty dream in which, as she tells Nelly in Chapter Nine, the angels fling her back to earth from a "heaven" which "did not seem to be my home", and she wakes on the heath "sobbing for joy": "I've no more business to marry Edgar Linton than I have to be in heaven."

Yet it is hardly surprising that the Grange does seem like "heaven" to the badly injured young girl who "sits quietly on the sofa" receiving her tributes of cakes and comforts. Her responsiveness to the different, infinitely more gracious possibilities for

life represented by the Grange is in part – like Pip's vision of Satis House in *Great Expectations* – a projection of hitherto unidentified, baffled needs, and of an emotional hunger that is all the more intense for being inchoate and unformulated.

For Michael Black, who rightly describes Heathcliff as a "conceivable human evolution", Catherine threatens to be "almost incomprehensible". But Catherine's cry – "I never did anything deliberately" – echoes through the novel because, wilful and selfish as she is, she never can understand what she is doing to herself and the two very young men who love her.

Given her nature and background, there is nothing whatever surprising in her first response to Thrushcross Grange. Neither she nor Heathcliff has seen anything like it, and it's worth noticing that Heathcliff's own response includes a kind of staggered, emotionally hungering awe, when he glimpses a world from which he is debarred. As he tells Nelly, after leaving Catherine behind at the Grange:

Both of us were able to look in by standing on the basement, and clinging to the ledge, and we saw –ah! it was beautiful – a splendid place carpeted with crimson, and crimson-covered chairs and tables, and a pure white ceiling bordered by gold, a shower of glass-drops hanging in silver chains from the centre, and shimmering with little soft

tapers. Old Mr. and Mrs. Linton were not there.
Edgar and his sister had it entirely to themselves;
shouldn't they have been happy? We should have
thought ourselves in heaven! (6)

Of course the young foundling Heathcliff is ejected
from this breathtaking world of luxury and
privilege, but Catherine – who comes from "the
next best house in the neighbourhood" – is not.
This creates, or simply reveals, an unexpected
division between young Heathcliff and the barefoot,
bleeding Catherine: after staying on at the Grange
for five weeks to convalesce, she finally returns to
the Heights as "a very dignified person with brown
ringlets falling from the cover of a feathered
beaver", "displaying fingers wonderfully whitened
with doing nothing, and staying indoors", and
exclaiming that Heathcliff, her soulmate, seems
"so dirty". Has she just been seduced – by material
luxuries?

That is what Terry Eagleton maintains in *Myths
of Power*, after presenting his generally persuasive
argument that "the choice posed for Catherine
between Heathcliff and Edgar Linton" is the
"pivotal event of the novel" and "the decisive
catalyst of the tragedy". If this is so, he goes on to
observe, "the crux of *Wuthering Heights* must
be conceded by even the most remorselessly
mythological and mystical of critics to be a social
one", in which "Cathy rejects Heathcliff as a suitor

because he is socially inferior to Linton". Her "choice" of a husband boils down to a choice between two homes, one of which will turn her into the neighbourhood's First Lady, while the other offers degradation and destitution. The Marxist Eagleton is predictably tough-minded about what this means, as a "perverse act of *mauvaise foi* [bad faith]" by which "Catherine trades her authentic selfhood for social privilege":

> She hopes to square authenticity with social convention, running in harness an ontological commitment to Heathcliff with a phenomenal relationship to Linton. "I am Heathcliff" is dramatically arresting, but it is also a way of keeping the outcast at arm's length, evading the challenge he offers. If Catherine is Heathcliff – if identity rather than relationship is in question – then their estrangement is inconceivable, and Catherine can therefore turn to others without violating the timeless metaphysical idea Heathcliff embodies.

More surprisingly, perhaps, Q.D. Leavis also inclines to the view that the first Catherine is "seduced" into entering "the artificial world of class, organised religion, social intercourse and authoritarian family life". As Leavis herself puts it, Catherine is "visibly" separated from her "natural" life, when "her inward succumbing to the temptations of superiority and riches parts her from Heathcliff". This is the point where it seems to me helpful to look ahead to *Great Expectations* (published in 1861) and Pip's first visit to Satis House. His imaginative horizons suddenly expand – like those of Catherine and Heathcliff on their first visit to the Grange: life, it seems, includes possibilities of which Pip and Catherine (and even Heathcliff) had never even dreamt, in their tiny and stultifyingly oppressive worlds of the forge and the Heights. The possibilities are imaginative, not merely material.

Unlike Dickens in *Great Expectations*, however, or Henry James in novels like *The Portrait of a Lady*, Brontë has no real interest in exploring what it really means to be a gentleman, and *Wuthering Heights*'s presentation of Edgar shows as much. If we ask whether Edgar has moral imagination in the Jamesean sense – whether he is "finely aware and richly responsible", or capable of "finely-tuned perceptions" – the answer is painfully clear: Edgar cannot really understand the girl he marries or his daughter, or the sister he coldly and resolutely abandons to her fate. Unlike Pip, he would be quite incapable of recognising a Magwitch or even Joe as human beings. He expects respect as his entitlement, and indeed deserves it in human terms; yet he is incapable of seeing how respect is something that must be earned, so that his distinction between who must be received in the kitchen or in the parlour is merely external and mechanical.

Yet in the novel's second half Edgar emerges as a humanly impressive character. He lacks anything like Heathcliff's passion, but he is devoted to his wife and their only child; when his wife dies and his daughter is lost to him Edgar dies inside, although, like Heathcliff, he goes on living for many years. As another study of continuing grief Edgar's case becomes very moving.

Nor is there any suggestion in the novel that Catherine doesn't love him or have a perfectly happy sexual relationship with him. Critics like Terry Eagleton – and in this respect Leavis – are too severe when they write of Catherine being "seduced" by the meretricious values of the Grange. Eagleton never once reflects that the woman he arraigns like a Grand Inquisitor for her "mauvaise foi" or "bad faith" is only a 12-year-old girl when she first visits the Grange, and only 15 when she determines to marry Edgar. The novel provides a psychologically convincing and coherent view of her arrested emotional and sexual development, and of what Heathcliff calls her "infernal selfishness". Michael Black finds Catherine unsatisfactory, but she seems to me just as "conceivable" a "human evolution" as Heathcliff or Hindley, and her marriage to Edgar wholly plausible.

What should we make of Catherine's "Nelly, I am Heathcliff!" speech?

The 15-year-old Catherine claims that she is Heathcliff in Chapter Nine, when she has determined to marry Edgar Linton but admits to having an "uneasy conscience". She then wants the unsympathetic Nelly to understand how much her love for Heathcliff means to her, and famously explains:

> *My great miseries in this world have been Heathcliff's miseries, and I watched and felt each from the beginning; my great thought in living is himself. If all else perished, and he remained, I should still continue to be; and if all else remained, and he were annihilated, the Universe would turn to a mighty stranger. I should not seem a part of it. My love for Linton is like the foliage in the woods: time will change it, I'm well aware, as winter changes the trees. My love for Heathcliff resembles the eternal rocks beneath: a source of little visible delight, but necessary. Nelly, I am Heathcliff! (9)*

As Jay Clayton puts it in his thoughtful 1987 study, *Romantic Vision and the Novel*, "Nelly, I am

Heathcliff!" may well be "the most famous expression of love in the whole course or the English novel", since "Catherine and Heathcliff call to mind the most notable romantic pairs in myth and literature: Orpheus and Eurydice, Romeo and Juliet, Tristram and Iseult".

Maybe so, yet it would never occur to the 14-year-old Juliet to say: "Nurse, I *am* Romeo." And there is no indication at all in this speech that the love Catherine feels for Heathcliff is sexual or romantic.

Clayton himself addresses this difficulty in his book when he observes that the "moment when [Heathcliff and Catherine] are first divided can be located with precision" in the "fully described" first visit to Thrushcross Grange, but we never see a "moment of union". Instead, there is what Clayton calls a "representational void". Catherine's unchanging love for Heathcliff begins when she is only six years old, as Nelly discovers in Chapter Five when she returns from her temporary banishment:

When Nelly finally returns "a few days afterwards" she finds that Catherine and Heathcliff "were now very thick". In the gap between these two sentences lies the birth of love. There is no other place to look because the novel makes no subsequent attempt to trace motives or find explanations. We can count on the fingers of one hand (and not need the thumb) the references to their bond that occur before the pressure of their separation elicits a compensatory force of response. The representational void is so great that William Wyler, making his [1939] movie of *Wuthering Heights*, felt required to fill it both with a place – Penistone Crags, where the lovers meet even after their death – and with an action, a sexual embrace.

John Matthews makes a similar point in "Framing in *Wuthering Heights*". Nelly's account of their childhood lives, he says, "invariably demonstrates that separation is the condition of their attraction, displacement the location of their alliance, exile the origin of their union". The pair often behave, indeed, "as if the barriers they take to separate themselves are the terms of their intimacy".

But if there is little justification for believing the love Catherine feels for Heathcliff is straightforwardly romantic, there is no reason to doubt the strength of her feeling for him, or to doubt that it matters more to her than anything else. The nature of that feeling is brilliantly shown in the metaphors she uses in her famous speech.

The speech, like the novel, works by offering two sets of contrasts. On the one hand, there are the contrasts between the Heights and the Grange, and the different potentialities for life each represents. On the other, there are the contrasts between Catherine's rival lovers, Heathcliff and

Edgar, and the different human potentialities they represent – above all, for Catherine, who must choose between them. The first set of contrasts is established through a range of solidly specific social and historical details, which correspond with those "realistic" and "sociological" aspects of the novel which Leavis rightly admires.

These contrasts are drawn in such an astonishingly sustained way that it is hard to think of parallels, although one would be with the no less astonishing way in which Shakespeare sustains the contrasts between "Egypt" and "Rome" in *Antony and Cleopatra* when presenting that play's protagonists and the different environments which shape them.

Consider some familiar and important examples. Edgar's portrait shows a cultivated, "pensive and amiable" man, "almost too graceful", who "wanted spirit in general"; whereas Heathcliff is, as Catherine tells Isabella, "an unreclaimed creature, without refinement, without cultivation, an arid wilderness of furze and whinstone". So just as Catherine associates Edgar with "foliage, surface change, and frivolous external things", and then associates Heathcliff with the "eternal rocks beneath", Nelly associates Edgar with a "beautiful fertile valley" and Heathcliff with "bleak, hilly coal country" – where, as Lockwood observes, "people do live more in earnest, more in themselves".

Like the other Lintons, Edgar has "vacant blue

eyes", eyes in which Catherine alone can kindle "a spark of spirit"; Heathcliff has "black eyes", "basilisk eyes", "eyes full of black fire", and the two men are as different as "a moonbeam from lightning, or frost from fire". The "soil" of the cultivated Edgar's "shallow cares" is opposed to the "flinty gratification" offered by Heathcliff's "half-civilised ferocity". The altruistic Edgar – of whom Catherine observes, "I believe I might kill him, and he wouldn't wish to retaliate" – is likened to a cat and a "sucking leveret", while Heathcliff is a "fierce, wolfish, pitiless man". Catherine figures in similar metaphorical contrasts when Nelly compares her with the (repelling) "thorn" and Edgar with the (clinging) "honeysuckle", or when Catherine returns from her convalescence at the Grange transformed from "a wild hatless savage" into a "very dignified person" with "fingers wonderfully whitened by doing nothing".

Such metaphorical contrasts can then be recycled when presenting the second generation, for example in the numerous contrasts between the effete Linton and the robust Hareton, or between the second Catherine's dream of happiness and Linton's: hers is joyously active whereas Linton's is passive and sickly, although neither has the stronger energies of the first generation.

The novel's use of so-called "metaphorical transfer" – with the characters taking on the same

TEN FACTS
ABOUT *WUTHERING HEIGHTS*

1.

Wuthering Heights was the only novel published by Emily Brontë.

2.

Originally published under the gender-neutral pseudonym "Ellis Bell", it was not until after Emily's death that Charlotte republished the novel under Emily's real name. The posthumous edition of *Wuthering Heights* published by Charlotte in 1850 included an introduction hailing the work as superior to her own novel *Jane Eyre*.

3.
The prototypes for Catherine and Heathcliff's characters were originally concocted in Emily's tale "cursed Zamorna" from the legend "Gondal", a work forged from the imaginary world of her childhood.

4.
The family surname Brontë is in fact a fiction, adapted by the sisters' father Patrick from the Irish surname "Brunty" to sound more impressive.

5.
Emily only received a total of 18 months' worth of formal education, including nine months at the Pensionnat Heger in Brussels. The rest of her education she received at home, preferring to spend her time amongst nature on the Yorkshire moors.

6.
She had a will of iron – after being bitten by a (possibly) rabid dog she is said to have walked calmly into the kitchen and cauterized the wound herself with a hot iron. When her brother Branwell wrapped himself in a blanket and set it on fire in a drunken stupor, Emily put out the flames with her bare hands.

7.

A solitary soul eschewing the company of strangers, Emily only spent six months of her adult life working at the Law Hill School near Halifax as a teacher. One of her students at this time recalled Emily telling the class that the school dog was dearer to her than her students.

8

There have been a total of 15 adaptations of *Wuthering Heights* for television and cinema since 1920, including a 1966 Hindi adaptation *Dil Diya Dard Liya* which takes the tale from the Yorkshire Moors to Bollywood Broadway. Laurence Olivier received his first Oscar nomination playing Heathcliff in Wyler's 1939 production of Wuthering Heights.

9.

After becoming ill with what turned into tuberculosis at her brother's funeral in September 1848, Emily refused to rest and rejected all medical help, saying she would have no "poisoning doctor" near her.

10.
Wuthering Heights became a UK number 1 hit single in 1979 after Kate Bush – who shares her birthday with Emily Brontë – adapted and expanded several of Catherine Earnshaw's quotations.

Juliette Binoche as Cathy Linton and Jason Riddington as Hareton Earnshaw in a 1992 film of Wuthering Heights

qualities as their environments – extends to involve plants and animals. As Catherine and Heathcliff see when they first peer through one of windows of the Grange, the children there have pets, whereas, as Lockwood unhappily discovers, animals in the Heights are either working animals or dead. The Grange has gardens and gardeners, whereas the hard, shared work of subsistence farming at the Heights involves making practical use of moorland. An orchard in the Grange is primarily there for the "visible delight" it affords the family, not because it is "necessary". At the Heights the currant bushes are there for food, just as cats are there to catch vermin. This contrast leads to subtle irony when the southern Frances arrives at the Heights: her warm responsiveness tells for her, though in fact she takes a predominantly aesthetic delight in household arrangements that are wholly practical and functional. The same contrast explains Joseph's apoplectic but profound horror when Hareton and Cathy pull up some of the currant bushes to make room for a flowerbed.

The metaphorical transfers in Catherine's speech all work to distinguish, in a Wordsworthian way, between Nature and Society, between the more and the less authentic, between the shallow and the deep, between the ephemeral and the permanent, between the agreeable and the necessary. Catherine's metaphorical contrast between "foliage" and the "eternal rocks beneath" obviously insists on the greater depth of her love for Heathcliff. At the same time the very power of her metaphorical contrasts encourages us *not* to ask what her love for Heathcliff actually is, and means, in non-metaphorical terms – and how it could ever be compatible with her unswerving determination to marry Edgar.

Q.D. Leavis answers that last question, correctly in my view, by arguing that Catherine's love for Heathcliff is "sibling" not "sexual". (Edgar suggests they are all but siblings when he pouts to Catherine about "the sight of your welcoming a runaway servant as a brother".) Of course the love in question is astonishingly intense, like Maggie Tulliver's feelings for her brother Tom in George Eliot's *The Mill on the Floss*. But when Catherine insists that her union with Heathcliff has never changed since she was six years old, her passionate affirmation also hints at some kind of arrested development. As a child and as an adult – although she doesn't survive beyond her teens – the first Catherine is never able to imagine other people's lives or feelings, or the ways in which, say, her own brother's needs might have been balked or thwarted. She cannot imagine what, in *Middlemarch*, George Eliot calls another person's "equivalent centre of self", and what the Russian critic Mikhail Bakhtin would call the "world of other consciousnesses with rights equal to those of the hero". Leavis puts it differently. Catherine is destroyed, she says, by a "fatal immaturity".

This arrested development, or "fatal immaturity", is very clear in the "I *am* Heathcliff!" speech. It is striking that both Catherine and so many critics in their excited commentaries seem unable to imagine Heathcliff as an independent character. To Keith Sagar, for example, he can only be understood as a "semi-mythical force":

Any attempt to 'explain' Heathliff in realistic terms seems to me futile. One of the most striking features of the novel is precisely Emily Brontë's refusal to provide any such explanations, her

HEATHCLIFF'S LANGUAGE

Heathcliff, like Catherine, speaks in his own distinctive way. His characteristically forceful metaphors in Chapter 14 are typical, as he compares his passion for Catherine with that of her "puny" husband's devotion to his wife. The metaphors leave no doubt that he thinks of himself as Catherine's proper mate and of Edgar as a contemptible rival lover:

If he loved with all the powers of his puny being, he couldn't love as much in eighty years, as I could in a day. And Catherine has a heart as deep as I have; the sea could as readily be contained in a horse trough, as her

determination that the reader shall be unable to account for Heathcliff in purely human terms.

Sagar goes on to claim that Catherine is "speaking literally when she says that she is Heathcliff" since there is "a sense in which Heathcliff does not function as an independent character at all, but as a projection of a part of Cathy's own being":

He is that within herself which is able to reach out and touch and be at one with the primary energies of nature: he is the root of her being.

In *The Female Imagination*, Patricia Spacks, a

---

whole affection be monopolised by him -- Tush! (14)

Or again:

He might as well plant an oak in a flower-pot, and expect it to thrive, as imagine he can restore her to vigour in the soil of his shallow cares! (14)

Heathcliff also refers to his "moral teething" – a very striking metaphor – when he so vehemently rejects Edgar's "duty and humanity", his "pity and charity". How should this be understood? It is a crucial moment, since Heathcliff is suddenly rejecting all of those social, altruistic and traditionally Christian virtues that would qualify Edgar to be a hero in a more conventional novel.

Heathcliff's metaphors involve natural forces that cannot be constrained in some socially acceptable but artificial way. Edgar's social and altruistic virtues don't

more hard-headed critic, is also content to take her cue from Catherine in writing as though Heathcliff had no independent existence:

> Heathcliff is partly a figment of Catherine's imagination... if he were not there she would have to invent him. In fact she does invent him, directly and indirectly shaping his being.

The theoretically sophisticated J. Hillis Miller, who insists that "what Catherine is to Heathcliff, Heathcliff is to Catherine", devotes several pages of *The Disappearance of God* to explaining why the "crucial sentence of *Wuthering Heights* is

---

just disgust him, they hurt him as a baby hurts when its teeth are coming through: hence his "moral teething" metaphor, which is anything but Wordsworthian. It's much closer to Blake's Proverbs of Hell in its power to shock – like Blake's proverb "Better murder an infant in its cradle than nurse unacted desires", which so shocked the French philosopher Simone Weil.

Both Heathcliff's and Blake's metaphors are asserting the absurdity, as well as the danger, of trying to constrain immense natural energies or forces. Yet as soon as we ask what Heathcliff is positively for, not merely virulently against, his use of the word "moral" becomes problematic. When he compares himself with Edgar his metaphors insist on his greater capacity for intense and violent passion without making it clear in what positive sense this constitutes a moral difference ∎

Catherine's bold expression of the paradox of substance: 'Nelly, I *am* Heathcliff'". And yet, for all his elaborate theories, Hillis Miller never once asks whether Catherine's assertion of identity might not be regarded as a perversion in its wilful denial of the loved one's otherness. That would help to account for Catherine's apparently contradictory outburst in Chapter 15, when Heathcliff criticises her "infernal selfishness" and she furiously exclaims: "That is not my Heathcliff!"

This apparent contradiction finds an odd but interesting parallel in the steadfast refusals of these critics to consider Heathcliff as an independent fictional character. In this respect Michael Black is exceptional in his claim that "Heathcliff can be understood, if we ever understand anybody... So far from being a mysterious semi-mythical force, he is presented with some care as a humanly conceivable evolution." None of the characters who tell their stories in *Wuthering Heights* understand this "lonely, suffering and violent man", but their incomprehension of him "is one of the things which the book allows *us* to grasp and understand". Catherine herself is too narcissistic to understand him. "In effect, Cathy wants to have it all," says Pauline Nestor, "an impulse that recalls what Freud has characterised as the polymorphous perversity of the infant." She thinks, like a child, that she must be loved – as she revealingly admits in Chapter 12.

"How strange! I thought, though everybody hated and despised each other, they could not avoid loving me."

What is troublingly clear in Catherine's case, although her metaphors in her "I *am* Heathcliff" speech mask or conceal the difficulty in question, is that she never feels or even wants intense sexual passion. Although her continuing need for Heathcliff encourages many readers to suppose that in her marriage to Edgar she never feels fully mated, there is nothing to suggest that she wants Heathcliff as a husband or mate in any sexual sense, or that the novel is a Regency version of *Lady Chatterley's Lover*. When Catherine says she wants to be "rich" and would like to be "the greatest woman of the neighbourhood" she is evidently drawn towards Society in a way that Heathcliff never is. Her feelings for "my Heathcliff" are – whether we find them obscurely impressive or obscurely regressive – quite unlike his agonisingly frustrated natural and sexual feelings for her. Cathy's infantile longings, Pauline Nestor rightly argues, are "the very opposite of mature sexuality", and when Edgar confronts her with the adult choice she must make – "Will you give up Heathcliff hereafter, or will you give up me?" – it is significant that she collapses, then declines into madness and death.

CRITICS ON EMILY BRONTË

"Wuthering Heights *has no mythology beyond what these two characters [Heathcliff and Catherine] provide: no great book is more cut off from the universals of Heaven and Hell. It is local, like the spirits it engenders, and whereas we may meet Moby Dick in any pond, we shall only encounter them among the harebells and limestone of their own county.*"

From E.M. Forster, *Aspects of the Novel*, 1927

[Emily Brontë] possessed "*a secret power and fire that might have informed the brain and kindled the veins of a hero... Stronger than a hero, simpler than a child, her nature stood alone.*"

Charlotte Brontë, *Biographical Notice of Ellis and Acton Bell*, 1850

"*She should have been a man – a great navigator... Her powerful reason would have deduced new spheres of discovery from the knowledge of the old; and her strong imperious will would never have been daunted by opposition or difficulty: never have given way but with life.*"

M. Heger, her Belgian teacher, 1857

How seriously should we take the violence in *Wuthering Heights?*

Although the first reviews of *Wuthering Heights* were by no means as uniformly hostile as Charlotte Brontë maintained in her 1850 Preface, many reviewers were shocked by the physical violence in the novel. And yet the violence is described with curious detachment and often seems scarcely real; much of it, remarks Q.D. Leavis, is "unrealised". Consider, for example, Heathcliff's account in Chapter Six, when he is about 13, of what happens when he and Catherine first go to the Grange. After they are detected they try to make their escape, but it is too late:

> *I had Cathy by the hand, and was urging her on, when all at once she fell down.*
> *"Run, Heathcliff, run!" she whispered. "They have let the bull-dog loose, and he holds me!"*

The watchdog Skulker has seized Catherine's foot, and since a bulldog's short-jawed bite is terribly tenacious there is a likelihood that she may be hamstrung or, as Mrs Linton puts it when she sees the bleeding foot, "lamed for life". Heathcliff tells Nelly how the dog had to be "throttled off, his huge, purple tongue hanging half a foot out of his mouth, and his pendant lips streaming with bloody slaver". That piles on the lurid effects – is any bulldog's tongue "half a foot"? – and yet the most extraordinary word in Heathcliff's account of all of this is "whispered". Does the 12-year-old Catherine even *feel* the terrible thing that has happened to her? Heathcliff is wanting to emphasise her extraordinary courage: "She did not yell out – no!"

Just as young Catherine barely seems to feel what has happened at the Grange, Isabella doesn't seem to feel physical pain in Chapter 17 when the maddened Heathcliff finally "snatched a dinner knife from the table, and flung it at my head". When the knife strikes Isabella it goes in deeply enough to stick into her neck, so that she has to pull it out. There is some sense of real physical damage when Isabella herself notices how the "deep cut" under her ear starts to bleed again, once she is in the warmth of the Grange: "ah – see how it flows down my neck now. The fire does make it smart." Yet Isabella's account of what happened seems almost impassive:

> It struck me beneath my ear, and stopped the sentence I was uttering; but pulling it out, I sprang to the door, and delivered another which I hope went a little deeper than his missile. (17)

This doesn't suggest the terrible, often traumatic

shock and sense of violation from which victims of domestic violence sometimes never recover. Although the *event* is striking and horrible in its external details, there is little sense of Isabella's suffering real pain when the knife lodged "beneath my ear", just as there is little sense of young Catherine's pain when she *whispers* that the bulldog has her foot.

Nelly's response, when Hindley is trying to force his knife between her teeth and down her throat, is also curiously impassive:

> *He held the knife in his hand, and pushed its point between my teeth: but, for my part, I was never much afraid of his vagaries. I spat it out, and affirmed it tasted detestably – I would not take it on any account. (9)*

Elsewhere, there is little sense of the all too often irreparable damage that can be caused by shaking a child until its teeth rattle, or of the lasting physical damage that might be done to the young Heathcliff when the vengeful Hindley and the Christian sadist Joseph beat him several times a week until their arms ache. I take it that this is what Leavis has in mind when she observes that much of the violence in the book is "unrealised".

The most shocking, unforgettable violence occurs in Chapter Three, when the terrified Lockwood seizes the wailing child-ghost's frozen hand and "pulled its wrist on to the broken pane, and rubbed it to and fro till the blood ran down and soaked the bedclothes". Terence McCarthy observes that it is the "polite, civilised gentleman" (and southerner) Lockwood who shows himself "capable, albeit in a dream, of greater cruelty than any of the savage inhabitants of Wuthering Heights".

Similarly, in her excellent feminist essay on *Wuthering Heights,* Naomi Jacobs observes that most of the violence in the novel, and in Anne Brontë's *The Tenant of Wildfell Hall,* is inflicted by men with money and power on women and children. She goes on to observe, tellingly, that Heathcliff himself, "the Liverpool orphan, commits his worst crimes only after he has acquired the manners and resources of a gentleman", but she by no means argues that men in general are necessarily more violent than women and she explores an important contrast between the Brontë sisters:

Unlike Charlotte, whose novels also critiqued the myth of domestic bliss but who eroticised the very dominance/submission dynamic from which she longed to escape, Emily and Anne seem to have moved beyond any faith in categories of gender as formulated by their culture. To them, gender is a ragged and somewhat ridiculous masquerade concealing the essential sameness of men and women.

But even though Lockwood's cruelty in Chapter Three shows what he and, by implication, all of us, however civilised, have it in us to become, it would be absurd to wonder whether what he does *hurts* the ghost-child, in the way that Catherine and Isabella must be, but don't seem to be, terribly hurt by the bulldog and the kitchen knife. What really hurts the real not ghostly children in this novel, and warps or, to use the novel's word, *mars* their development like that of the twisted firs, is the absence or withdrawal of love.

And what so devastates the pregnant Isabella after her marriage, and after 18 years of being

ISABELLA

So far as the dark, cruelly incisive comedy in Chapter 17 is concerned, it works entirely at the expense of poor, dim Isabella. Perhaps for that reason critics usually ignore it, but I would challenge any reader to read the following breathlessly melodramatic sentence aloud without smiling:

On my flight through the kitchen I bid Joseph speed to his master; I knocked over Hareton, who was hanging a litter of puppies from a chair-back in the doorway; and, blest as a soul escaped from purgatory, I bounded, leaped, and flew down the steep road; then, quitting its windings, shot direct across the moor, rolling over banks, and wading through marshes; precipitating myself, in fact, towards the beacon light of the Grange. (17)

pampered at the Grange, is the traumatic discovery that her husband does not love her, but despises her, and her continuing confusion about whether she might still, somehow, continue to love him. Her feelings for Heathcliff keep swivelling to and fro in an adolescent but genuinely painful way:

> I've recovered from my first desire to be killed by him. I'd rather he killed himself! He has extinguished my love effectually, and so I'm at my ease. I can recollect yet how I loved him, and can dimly imagine that I could still be loving him, if – No, no! (17)

The first part of the sentence, describing the commotion Isabella causes in the kitchen when she finally escapes from the Heights, wouldn't be out of place in *Cold Comfort Farm*, Stella Gibbons's very funny satire on the "rural" melodrama of writers like Mary Webb. The glimpse of Hareton's curiously sadistic exercise before Isabella knocks him over is far more likely to prompt a smile than a shudder: why on earth should he be "hanging a litter of puppies from a chair-back in the doorway" instead of drowning them or breaking their necks? The rest of the sentence, describing Isabella's flight to the Grange, looks forward to Peter York's cruelly funny *Sloane Ranger's Handbook*, in which York noticed how "Sloanes" always preferred to choose exaggerated, would-be dramatic verbs to describe their largely insignificant activities.

Like the "Sloanes", Isabella can't simply walk or run anywhere. She "bounded, leaped, and flew" down the road, before she "shot direct" across the

Isabella's gravest injury is caused not by the kitchen knife, but by the struggle to understand that the man she loves does not love her. This, I think, is one of the novel's most profound and original insights.

It is clear, too, if we consider how Hindley and Heathcliff are, in an important sense, complementary figures. They become the two most violent men in the novel, the latter's violence prompting Charlotte Brontë famously to doubt whether it is "right or advisable to create beings like [him]". As the strongest character in the novel,

---

moor, "precipating myself, in fact". That "in fact" is delicious, and perfectly placed after the ludicrous verb "precipitating"; a modern version of Isabella would probably speak of precipitating herself "literally". Of course Brontë isn't lapsing into melodramatic, novelettish writing; she is showing and enjoying the dizzy ways in which Isabella constantly casts herself as the heroine in her own tripey melodrama. Indeed, we are being given important clues about the young, privileged and anything but bright

Isabella's taste for popular "Romantic" and "Gothic" reading matter – which had so much to do with her initial attraction to the darkly Byronic Heathcliff, whom she supposed must just love her once he had discovered her non-existent charms.

Heathcliff suggests as much in Chapter 14, when he sneeringly refers to Isabella's "delusion" in "forming a fabulous notion of my character" and "picturing in me a hero of romance". Isabella's real agony, after being privileged and pampered through the whole of her earlier life, is

whose powers of endurance seem almost unlimited, Heathcliff becomes the foremost example of how, the withdrawal or absence of love is far more damaging than physical violence.

Nelly recalls that, on the day he left the Heights and disappeared for more than three years, Heathcliff "had reached the age of sixteen then, I think". He had been a victim of violence, never an agent, since his arrival at the Heights nine years earlier – and probably, as Nelly also guesses, for much longer. She notes how he "seemed a sullen, patient child" who had already been "hardened,

that she cannot believe that she is not loved by the "incarnate goblin" she still loves. Even when she throws her wedding ring into the Grange fireplace she says to Nelly, who sees her dropping the "misused article among the coals" as an example of her "childish spite": "There! He shall buy me another, if he gets me back again."

So when she describes how this "incarnate goblin" looked through the window, or, rather, how "his black countenance looked blightingly through" it, and how his "hair and clothes were whitened with snow, and his sharp cannibal teeth, revealed by cold and wrath, gleamed through the dark", we would be being as fancifully silly as Isabella if we supposed that Heathcliff really has peculiarly sharp and magically luminous "cannibal teeth", like Edward Lear's Dong with a Luminous Nose. That is just how Isabella sees her make-believe world. As Michael Black notes, such things "are all in the reporting". Yet the comedy in question is tragi-comic, because it involves so much real pain – hers, as well as Heathcliff's ∎

perhaps, to ill treatment". When he was being beaten up by young Hindley, twice his age and size, he "would stand Hindley's blows without winking or shedding a tear", and Nelly describes how her own pinches "moved him only to draw in a breath and open his eyes, as if he had hurt himself by accident and nobody was to blame".

This dreadful situation only eases when Heathcliff is about ten, and Hindley is packed off to college. Three years later, it becomes even more unbearable, and dangerous, when old Earnshaw dies and Hindley returns to become the new "master" of the Heights. Not only does Hindley, now 20 and far more powerful, turn the 13-year-old Heathcliff out of the house as a stable-boy, he separates him from Catherine and makes him the victim of far more savage beatings in which Joseph readily takes over when the new master's arm is tired.

Indeed, Heathcliff is then subjected to the *systematic* degradation that Terry Eagleton describes very perceptively in *Myths of Power*, when he notes how, from the first, Heathcliff's arrival twists "all the Earnshaw relationships into bitter antagonism":

He unwittingly sharpens a violence endemic to the Heights – a violence which springs both from the hard exigencies imposed by its struggle with the land, and from its social exclusiveness as a self-consciously ancient, respectable family. The violence which Heathcliff unconsciously triggers is turned against him: he is cast out by Hindley, culturally deprived, reduced to the status of farm-labourer. What Hindley does, in fact, is to invert the potential freedom symbolised by Heathcliff into a parody of itself, into the non-freedom of neglect. Heathcliff is robbed of liberty in two antithetical ways: exploited as a servant on the one hand, allowed to run wild on the other; and this contradiction is appropriate to childhood, which is a time of relative freedom from convention and yet, paradoxically, a time of authoritarian repression.

In this sense there is freedom for Heathcliff neither within society nor outside it: his two conditions are inverted mirror-images of one another. It is a contradiction which encapsulates a crucial truth about bourgeois society. If there is no genuine liberty on its 'inside' – Heathcliff is oppressed by work and the familial structure – neither is there more than a caricature of liberty on the 'outside', since the release of running wild is merely a function of cultural impoverishment. The friendship of Heathcliff and Cathy crystallises under the pressures of economic and cultural violence, so that the freedom it seems to signify ("half-savage and hardy, and free") is always the other face of oppression...

All of this might seem unendurable, but Heathcliff

survives it for three years – until he hears Catherine confide to Nelly that it "would degrade me to marry Heathcliff now". This apparent withdrawal of love is unendurable, and Heathcliff leaves the Heights at once.

What makes Heathcliff plot revenge?

Chapter Four finishes with the account of how, when Mr Earnshaw was still alive, he "once bought a couple of colts at the parish fair, and gave the lads each one": as Earnshaw's favourite, Heathcliff could choose, and "took the handsomest". But then, when his horse falls lame, young Heathcliff announces to Hindley:

> *"You must exchange horses with me: I don't like mine, and if you won't I shall tell your father of the three thrashings you've given me this week, and show him my arm, which is black to the shoulder." (4)*

The furious Hindley cuffs Heathcliff's ears, and then pursues him to the porch, threatening him with "an iron weight used for weighing potatoes and hay". When Heathcliff persists in his demand, Hindley throws the iron weight, "hitting him on the breast, and down he fell, but staggered up immediately, breathless and white". Nelly stops him from going "just so to the master", and getting "full revenge". The anguished, much stronger but helpless young Hindley says:

> *"Take my colt, gipsy, then! And I pray that he may break your neck: take him, and be damned, you beggarly interloper! and wheedle my father out of all he has: only afterwards show him what you are, imp of Satan. – And take that, I hope he'll kick out your brains!"*

Hindley then knocks the younger child under the horse's feet, and, as Nelly recalls with some contempt, runs away "as fast he could", without "waiting to see whether his hopes were fulfilled".

The chapter ends with a final twist. Nelly watches as the hurt Heathcliff once again

> *gathered himself up, and went on with his intention; exchanging saddles and all, and then sitting down on a bundle of hay to overcome the qualm which the violent blow occasioned, before entering the house.*
>
> *I persuaded him easily to let me lay the blame of his bruises on the horse: he minded little what tale was told since he had what he wanted. He complained so seldom, indeed, of such stirs as these, that I really thought him not vindictive: I was deceived completely, as you will hear.*

What would our response be, if Nelly had not added those last words, so that the chapter had ended with "I really thought him not vindictive"? But Nelly's judgement is harsh, and we ourselves are being tempted to judge him more harshly than perhaps we should.

Heathcliff has evidently never shown his bruises to old Earnshaw before, and Nelly can "easily" persuade him not to do so now – once he has "what he wanted". He is used to being "ill-used" and never complains on his own behalf, although Nelly ascribes this to his natural "hardness" not to any "soft", tender or moral propensity. Leavis describes the Heathcliff we see in this episode as a "vicious, scheming and morally heartless – 'simply insensible' – boy". In her view, this boy Heathcliff is of course not assimilable with the Heathcliff who roams the countryside with Catherine in idyllic and innocent happiness. But her view of the vicious, "Edmund-like" boy seems exaggerated to me.

Similarly I think we should remember that Heathcliff is only 12 or 13 when he describes the momentous first visit to Thrushcross Grange to Nelly and mentions what he longs to do to Hindley and Joseph:

> *"I'd not exchange, for a thousand lives, my condition here, for Edgar Linton's at Thrushcross Grange – not even if I might have the privilege of flinging Joseph off the highest*

Ralph Fiennes as Heathcliff in the 1992 television adaptation

gable, and painting the house-front with Hindley's blood!" (6)

In part this is the spirited compensatory fantasy of a boy who cannot stop the now more powerful, manly Hindley from beating him regularly. After the fateful visit to the Grange the degraded Heathcliff is not flogged again. Instead, and far worse, Hindley warns him that "the first word" he speaks to "Miss Catherine" will "ensure a dismissal".

Years later, when Heathcliff comes back "into the country", he appears to have no definite plan for revenge and Joseph's name is not on what could now be called his hit-list. Only one name is – Hindley's. As he tells Catherine and Edgar:

"I heard of your marriage, Cathy, not long since; and, while waiting in the yard below, I meditated this plan: just to have one glimpse of your face, a stare of surprise, perhaps, and pretended pleasure; afterwards settle my score with Hindley; and then prevent the law by doing execution on myself." (10)

He is evidently determined to take revenge on Hindley, but not for the violence inflicted on him by Hindley and Joseph. He is entirely indifferent to his own past sufferings, and when he becomes the new "master" at the Heights he does not even dismiss Joseph. But Hindley must be destroyed for launching the reign of terror in which Heathcliff is separated from Catherine and degraded to the point where Catherine herself feels that it would "degrade me to marry Heathcliff now". At this stage there is certainly no "plan" to bring down both houses, and it is misleading to describe the returned Heathcliff as, in John Sutherland's phrase, a "gentleman psychopath". As ever, Heathcliff lives and breathes only for Catherine.

Neither Catherine nor Edgar shows the least concern, or even interest, in the limited "plan" that Heathcliff describes. Catherine's lack of concern for her brother's looming fate is not surprising, since she has hated Hindley ever since she was six and grew "thick" with the boy her brother was constantly beating up; but her indifference to Heathcliff's "plan" to defeat the law by committing suicide is more startling, unless we reflect that her passion for "my Heathcliff" has little to do with the real, lonely and suffering man and more to do with her own ego. Edgar's complete lack of concern with whatever the "stable-boy" plans to do to the second most important gentleman in the neighbourhood is startling, if only because Edgar is also a magistrate.

But then we see nothing of Edgar in the three-year period between his proposal and his marriage, and what we do see, at first, of the adult, married Edgar in Chapter 10 suggests that the spoilt and privileged child has turned into the man who is and will always be a snob. When Heathcliff returns Edgar's chief concern appears to be that the "stable-boy" should be seen in the kitchen, not received in the parlour. In this respect the novel has yet to surprise us by showing how Edgar is a more impressive character than we imagined, how he loves his wife deeply, in his own way, and has "spirit" enough to punch Heathcliff in the throat.

Heathcliff's so far limited plan for revenge only begins to open out later in the same chapter, when Edgar is forced to leave the Grange to attend "a justice-meeting at the next town" and Heathcliff, "aware of his absence, called rather earlier than usual". Isabella has by now re-entered the novel as "a charming lady of eighteen; infantile in manners, though possessed of keen wit, keen feelings, and a keen temper too, if irritated". As Nelly shrewdly notes, her "master's uneasiness" over Heathcliff's visits to the Grange "experienced a lull" when there were no more "startling demonstrations of feeling" from Catherine – and when "further circumstances diverted it into another channel": "His new source of trouble sprang from the not anticipated misfortune of Isabella Linton evincing a sudden and irresistible attraction towards the tolerated guest."

Although Edgar attributes this development to "Heathcliff's deliberate designing", Nelly tells Lockwood that Edgar is mistaken about this: the "infantile" Isabella's novelettish infatuation "rose unsolicited, and was bestowed where it awakened no reciprocation of sentiment".

Catherine is, of course, furious with Isabella for falling in love, and for showing her "keen temper" when the two girls have their teenage quarrel: Isabella declares that she loves Heathcliff "more than you ever loved Edgar", and calls Catherine a "dog in the manger" who desires "no one to be loved" but herself. Catherine then bitterly humiliates Isabella by telling Heathcliff that Isabella is "breaking her heart by mere contemplation of your physical and moral beauty" and that it lies "in your own power to be Edgar's brother". Heathcliff scoffs, saying that he likes her "too ill to attempt it" and would be "turning the blue eyes black and blue". But then there is a pause, while Heathcliff considers this new turn.

> "She's her brother's heir, is she not?" he asked, after a brief silence.
> "I should be sorry to think so," returned his companion. "Half-a-dozen nephews shall erase her title, please Heaven. Abstract your mind from the subject, at present. You are too prone to covet your neighbour's goods: remember this neighbour's goods are mine."
> "If they were mine, they would be none the less that," said Heathcliff, "but though Isabella Linton may be silly, she is scarcely mad; and, in short, we'll dismiss the matter, as you advise."
>
> (10)

There is no reason to doubt the truth of Heathcliff's immediate and impressive remark that whatever is "mine" would be Catherine's. Nor is it difficult to imagine – although we are never told, and can only imagine – his inner agony when Catherine so cruelly says that "Half-a-dozen nephews" will "erase" Isabella's "title". Nelly, watching and hearing all of this, notes that they did "dismiss" the matter "from their tongues", and "Catherine, probably, from her thoughts". But the alarmed

Nelly is sure that Heathcliff "recalled it often in the course of the evening":

> *I saw him smile to himself – grin rather – and*
> *lapse into ominous musing whenever Mrs Linton*
> *had occasion to be absent from the apartment.*
> *I determined to watch his movements.*

"A plague on both your houses," says Shakespeare's dying Mercutio. Heathcliff's "plan" for a comprehensive or inclusive revenge, in which he will own and bring down both the Heights and the Grange, doesn't really evolve until long after he has married Isabella, after she has escaped and gone south to bear and look after their repellent son Linton, and then much more time has passed: like Shakespeare in *The Winter's Tale*, Brontë must allow years enough to pass for the second generation to grow up – and in this case Linton, Hareton and the second Catherine all grow up to become the victims of a man who could, by then, be justly described as a "gentleman psychopath".

What makes Heathcliff give up his plan?

We have no access to what is going on inside Heathcliff's mind until the end of Chapter 29, when he tells Nelly how he has struck one side of Catherine's coffin loose – "not Linton's side, damn him!" – and bribed the sexton to remove that and the adjacent side of his own coffin when he is buried beside her: "by the time Linton gets to us, he'll not know which is which!"

And then, suddenly and unexpectedly, Heathcliff tells Nelly what happened earlier, when he dug up Catherine's grave on the snowy night after her funeral. Before opening the coffin he heard a sigh behind him and "felt that Cathy was there, not under me, but on the earth":

Her presence was with me; it remained while I filled in the grave, and led me home. You may laugh, if you will, but I was sure I should see her there. I was sure she was with me, and I could not help talking to her.

Having reached the Heights, I rushed eagerly to the door. It was fastened; and, I remember, that accursed Earnshaw and my wife opposed my entrance. I remember stopping to kick the breath out of him, and then hurrying upstairs, to my room, and hers. I looked round impatiently – I felt her by me – I could almost

*see her, and yet I could not! I ought to have
sweat blood then, from the anguish of my
yearning, from the fervour of my supplications
to have but one glimpse! I had not one. She
showed herself, as she so often was in life, a devil
to me!*

*... And when I slept in her chamber – I was
beaten out of that – I couldn't lie there; for the
moment I closed my eyes, she was either outside
the window, or sliding back the panels, or
entering the room, or even resting her darling
head on the same pillow as she did when a child.
And so I opened and closed them a hundred times
a night – to be always disappointed! It racked
me!*

*...Now since I've seen her, I'm pacified – a
little. It was a strange way of killing, not by
inches, but by fractions of hair-breadths, to
beguile me with the spectre of a hope, through
eighteen years! (29)*

This is one of the novel's most remarkable
narrative "loops", since it loops back to Lockwood's
nightmare in Chapter Three and reveals the full
significance of the emphases in Heathcliff's
anguished outcry through the lattice window:

*"Come in! come in!" he sobbed. "Cathy, do come.
Oh, do–once more! Oh my heart's darling, hear
me this time – Catherine, at last!" (3)*

Through all the years since Catherine died on May 20, 1784, and since Heathcliff's curse or "prayer" in Chapter 16 that she would "haunt" him, her ghost has never "once" appeared until "this time" – that is, the night in late November 1801 when Lockwood has his dream, if it is a dream. Heathcliff's account of what happened on the night after her funeral also loops back to Isabella's account of how, when Heathcliff returned, he seemed so sunk in despair that she went on goading him more and more until he finally threw the knife at her. Now, 12 chapters later, we learn why Heathcliff was in such despair. Indeed so great was his despair that he does not even remember his wife's escape.

In Chapter 31, when Lockwood next visits the Heights, he overhears an important hint that Heathcliff is becoming less concerned to carry out his comprehensive revenge – with Cathy and Hareton as his final victims. Poor Hareton storms out of the house in "grief and anger" after being terribly tormented by Cathy, just as Heathcliff is coming up the causeway. Laying hold of Hareton's shoulder, Heathcliff asks in what is for him an almost tender way: "What's to do now, my lad?" But Hareton breaks away.

> Heathcliff gazed after him, and sighed. "It will be odd, if I thwart myself!" he muttered, unconscious that I was behind him. "But when I look for his father in his face, I find

her every day more! How the devil is he so like? I can hardly bear to see him." (31)

This is all the more moving because of the curious way in which Heathcliff almost recedes from much of the second half of the novel, even though he is in another sense controlling almost everything that happens. A telling Shakespearean analogy would be with the similarly curious effect of recession in Shakespeare's second historical tetralogy, when Prince Hal finally becomes Henry V. Then, whenever we see him, he is always performing as King – staging himself, as his father put it. He dominates almost every scene in the play, but the complicated man whom we have come to know as Prince Hal has almost disappeared from view and, as Gary Taylor cleverly says, can be glimpsed only through occasional "fissures".

The two brief passages in Chapters 29 and 31 are also like "fissures" through which we can glimpse what is happening inside Heathcliff, without that view being distorted by witnesses and victims who hate and misunderstand this lonely man. Then finally, when the romance between Cathy and Hareton has been brought to its happy conclusion in Chapter 32, Heathcliff opens his heart to Nelly in the two final chapters.

Once again, as he talks in these last chapters, we are reminded of Lockwood's "nightmare", which occurred just six months earlier in chronological terms. Heathcliff is, of course, convinced that this was no dream, and that Catherine's ghost has come "at last". During the last six months of his life he becomes ever more convinced that she is really haunting him. He keeps thinking he can see her at last, where the frightened Nelly can see nothing at all, and by now he has altogether lost interest in completing his revenge on the second generation. As he tells Nelly in Chapter 33:

> *"It is a poor conclusion, is it not," he observed... "An absurd termination to my violent exertions? I get levers and mattocks to demolish the two houses, and train myself to be capable of working like Hercules, and when everything is in my power, I find the will to lift a slate off either roof has vanished! My old enemies have not beaten me; now would be the precise time to revenge myself on their representatives: I could do it, and none could hinder me. But where is the use?*

Heathcliff then refers to the crisis which has taken place five minutes before, in which he seemed about to kill Cathy and Hareton begged him "not to hurt her". At that moment, says Heathcliff, Hareton "seemed a personification of my youth, not a human being":

> *I felt to him in such a variety of ways, that it*

would have been impossible to accost him rationally.

In the first place, his startling likeness to Catherine connected him fearfully with her. That, however, which you may suppose the most potent to arrest my imagination, is actually the least, for what is not connected with her to me? And what does not recall her? I cannot look down to this floor, but her features are shaped on the flags!... The entire world is a dreadful collection of memoranda that she did exist, and that I have lost her!

Well, Hareton's aspect was the ghost of my immortal love, of my wild endeavours to hold to my right, my degradation, my pride, my happiness, and my anguish...

I find this the most moving speech in the whole novel, from Heathcliff's piercing use of the wonderful phrase "I felt to him" to his heartrending account of how Hareton's "aspect" has come to seem like the "ghost" of his own younger self. We understand, now, the depth of the despair of this miserable and much wronged man and why he cannot carry out his revenge. There is an echo here, too, of the tenderness which Heathcliff shows in his final meeting with the Catherine he loves. When she begs him not to go, his response is: "Hush, my darling! Hush, hush, Catherine! I'll stay." These are "the only humanly consoling words he speaks in the book", says Michael Black:

> She needs him; he responds, glad to meet her last need. This meeting in fear and desolation – she terrified of being alone, he comforting her in her dread – is as near as they get to a union before the end of the book. It gives them their relative stature, he larger and potentially kinder than she.

Significantly, Hareton is devastated by Heathcliff's death when, finally, the narrative loop which began with Lockwood's nightmare ends with Nelly discovering Heathcliff's already stiff body (she can't close his eyes) under the same lattice window.

> *But poor Hareton, the most wronged, was the only one that really suffered much. He sat by the corpse all night, weeping in bitter earnest. He pressed its hand, and kissed the sarcastic, savage face that everyone else shrank from contemplating; and bemoaned him with that strong grief which springs naturally from a generous heart, though it be as tough as tempered steel. (34)*

How important is the supernatural in *Wuthering Heights?*

The "transgressive power" of *Wuthering Heights* is evident in all kinds of ways, says Pauline Nestor in her introduction to the Penguin edition. It is evident in the brutal violence. It is further evident in the novel's "flirtation with the fundamental taboos, especially those against incest and necrophilia". Heathcliff's readiness to defy taboos is evident in his yearning for Catherine's dead body – and while, strictly speaking, incest is never committed because Heathcliff and Cathy are not blood relations and their relationship is never consummated, "there is a quasi-incestuous element to their bond, given their upbringing as brother and sister".

The incest theme also "resonates" in the second half of *Wuthering Heights* in the intermarriages of the second generation, with Catherine marrying two cousins in succession.

The appearance of Cathy's ghost is equally unsettling, says Nestor, "challenging not only the limits of life, but those of reality".

Throughout *Wuthering Heights*, Brontë's treatment of the supernatural is subtle and ambiguous. Lockwood's terrible dream, if it is a dream, can be explained by the delirious state he is in when he goes to sleep. He has been soaked and frozen in fighting his way to the Heights through the icy blizzard. When he arrives he is attacked by dogs, then made woozy by alcohol after the shock of meeting an entirely unfamiliar lack of hospitality. He is excited, and upset. When he is finally granted a room in which to spend the night he finds the ponderous theological tome in which young Catherine has used the margins as a diary, and his head is soon swimming with the alternative names "Catherine Earnshaw", "Catherine Linton", "Catherine Heathcliff". The names seem to be "swarming in the air". And then there is the branch, endlessly tapping on the glass of the casement he cannot unhasp.

That last detail shows what care Brontë takes to provide alternative "explanations" to supernatural events. Lockwood mentions that the hook on the casement window had been "soldered into the staple" – "a circumstance observed by me, when awake, but forgotten". When the desperate Lockwood finally knocks his knuckles through the glass to seize and break the infernal tapping branch, his "fingers closed on the fingers of a little, ice-cold hand". Hearing the "most melancholy voice" sobbing, "Let me in – let me in!", he "discerned, obscurely, a child's face looking through the window". And then, in the novel's most horrifyingly violent moment, Lockwood pulls the child-ghost's wrist down and "rubs it against the broken glass of the window until the blood ran down and soaked the bedclothes". Is there really blood on the bedclothes? We are not told. But even if we were, we could not know whether the blood is that of a ghost – if ghosts can bleed – or Lockwood's own blood, after he has knocked out the glass with his knuckles.

When Lockwood cries out and Heathcliff arrives, he repeats his "ridiculous nightmare". Heathcliff violently dismisses Lockwood and then, while still within the narrator's earshot, tears open the soldered lattice and cries into the darkness: "Cathy, do come. Oh do – once more! Oh! my heart's darling, hear me this time – Catherine, at last!" As that unmistakably implies, Catherine has never yet "come", in all the years since her death. Heathcliff supposes that she may have come "this time", for the first time. Lockwood sardonically comments:

> *The spectre showed a spectre's ordinary caprice, it gave no sign of being; but the snow and wind whirled wildly through, even reaching my station, and blowing out the light. (3)*

But then in the final chapter – hundreds of pages later, though only months later in the novel's time-line – we remember Heathcliff's outcry when Nelly finds him under the same lattice window. She needs "another key" to open the room, since

Heathcliff has locked it. When she finally obtains "entrance" she discovers Heathcliff's corpse under the casement window:

> *Mr Heathcliff was there – laid on his back. His eyes met mine so keen, and fierce, I started; and then, he seemed to smile.*
>
> *I could not think him dead – but his face and throat were washed with rain; the bed-clothes dripped, and he was perfectly still. The lattice, flapping to and fro, had grazed one hand that rested on the sill – no blood trickled from the broken skin, and when I put my fingers to it, I could doubt no more – he was dead and stark!*
>
> *I hasped the window; I combed his black long hair from his forehead; I tried to close his eyes, to extinguish, if possible, that frightful, life-like gaze of exultation, before any one else beheld it. They would not shut – they seemed to sneer at my attempts, and his parted lips, and sharp, white teeth sneered too! (34)*

When Mr Kenneth, the doctor, finally arrives, he is "perplexed to pronounce of what disorder the master died". Nelly "conceals the fact of his having swallowed nothing for four days, fearing it might lead to trouble", and provides the last of her self-justifications for this judicious deceit: "I am persuaded he did not abstain on purpose; it was the consequence of his strange illness, not the cause."

Once again, the "supernatural" possibility is accompanied by a "natural" explanation that is not enough to satisfy Nelly. She affirms that Heathcliff's prolonged refusal to eat anything is "the consequence", not "the cause", of his "strange illness" or, as she also calls it, "monomania on the subject of his departed idol". Heathcliff's "life-like gaze of exultation", and his "girning" at death as the final release he will never allow himself until Catherine does at last return, show his conviction in the last days of his life that she has at last "come"

TALES OF HOFFMANN

Some Brontë scholars believe the sisters were familiar with the supernatural stories and poems of the Scottish writer James Hogg (1770-1835). Some follow Mary Ward in thinking that Emily, who studied German during her unhappy time in Brussels, was influenced by the German writer E.T.A. Hoffmann (pictured above).

For Ward, Emily Brontë was a highly conscious literary artist, and *Wuthering Heights* showed "the grafting of a European tradition upon a mind already richly stored". Hogg's most extraordinary work, *The Confessions of a Justified Sinner* (1824), provides what I take to be one precedent for the Brontës' treatment of the "supernatural". Just as the young Brontës had lapped up the local lore, tales and legends that they heard (in broad dialect) from Tabitha, the family housekeeper, so they would have enjoyed the best of

to find and take him. For Heathcliff this "monomania" becomes the only reality: the "entire world" has become "a dreadful collection of memoranda that she did exist, and that I have lost her". But once again the material for a "natural" explanation has been assembled. Nelly can't close Heathcliff's eyes because he has been dead for 24 hours, or longer than she thinks.

The same ambiguity is there in the final chapter when Lockwood goes to visit the graves "on the slope next the moor". Not long before this, we are told, Nelly is walking back to the Grange when she

---

Hogg's own supernatural ballads. *The Confessions of a Justified Sinner* is more complicated than these ballads, and, as Karl Miller notes in his fascinating book *Doubles*, clearly anticipates Stevenson's *Dr Jekyll and Mr Hyde*.

E.T.A. Hoffmann (1776-1822) was in another league. Not only were his "fantastic" tales acclaimed internationally, he was also a lawyer and a composer, who in 1816 was elevated to Berlin's Supreme Court and completed his opera *Undine*. He was also a theatre director and caricaturist, and a music critic and reviewer who wrote a remarkable essay on Mozart's *Don Giovanni* and some of the most perceptive reviews of Beethoven's works. In short, he was a great original.

His "fantastic" tales are sometimes very frightening. So, for example, his famous "Sandman" is a terrifying figure, who searches out naughty children and throws sand in their eyes with tremendous force until their eyeballs pop out. The Sandman then pops these into his sack and carries them off to feed to his

encounters a "little boy with a sheep and two lambs before him" who is "crying terribly". She asks him, "What is the matter, my little man?", and the weeping boy explains that he has just seen "Heathcliff and a woman, yonder, under t'Nab". Nelly reflects, in her characteristically sensible way, that he

probably raised the phantoms from thinking, as he traversed the moors, alone, on the nonsense he had heard his parents and companions repeat.
But soon after this common-sense rebuttal of any

---

beaked young. Add to this that the story is told by a frightened boy who fears that his father is behaving strangely, as though he had somehow been emasculated, and you don't need to be a psychologist to think that more is going on than meets the eye(ball).

But when Ward argues that Brontë was influenced by Hoffmann she never produces striking and specific parallels in the way that Q.D. Leavis does when she shows how *Wuthering Heights* was influenced by Walter Scott's novel *The Bride of Lammermoor* and

his story "The Black Dwarf". What Ward sees as an influence was probably more a significant affinity.

That seems all the more likely when we notice how all three sisters took care to set "supernatural" possibilities against "natural" alternatives. There is one famous exception. When Jane Eyre hears Rochester calling her name, although he is impossibly far away, this doesn't establish the supremacy of the supernatural. But then Charlotte believed that telepathy was a familiar natural occurrence ∎

supernatural possibility (where common sense is what tells us that the earth is flat) Nelly admits to Lockwood: "yet still, I don't like being out in the dark, now". When Lockwood half-jokes that this is the time the ghosts may "choose to inhabit" the Heights, she uneasily prevaricates:

> *"No, Mr Lockwood," said Nelly, shaking her head. "I believe the dead are at peace, but it is not right to speak of them with levity."*

The last paragraph of the novel is equally ambiguous, as Lockwood stands by the graves:

> *I lingered round them, under that benign sky: watched the moths fluttering among the heath and harebells, listened to the soft wind breathing through the grass, and wondered how any one could ever imagine unquiet slumbers for the sleepers in that quiet earth.*

Since the novel's Lockwood wants – or needs – to be more rational than his Hollywood counterpart, he brings his narration to a close by dismissing the phantoms as imaginary. How, he "wonders", could ghosts walk under that "benign sky", with the "soft wind" breathing – not wuthering – through the grass? Frank Kermode is siding with Lockwood's rationalist, terminal rather than radical scepticism when he almost snidely remarks that "Heathcliff's ghost and Catherine's, at the end, are of interest only to the superstitious, the indigenous now to be dispossessed by a more rational culture." This chimes with Kermode's comment that the Grange represents "a new world in the more civil south".

Kermode's view is too reassuring. The effect of having Lockwood wonder "how any one could ever imagine" that these "sleepers" could still "walk" the moors, as the locals maintain, is that we once again consider and "imagine" the very possibility that Lockwood wants to dismiss – or, as his very name suggests, lock out. Emily Brontë is always careful to provide possible rational ways of seeing what her characters experience; indeed all of the novels by the Three Weird Sisters (as Ted Hughes wickedly christened them, recalling *Macbeth*) tackle the so-called supernatural in this way, taking care to provide alternative explanations for supposedly "supernatural" events. But it is impossible to know what Emily Brontë thought about the supernatural – the same is true of Shakespeare – and in a novel which suggests that so much of our lives is controlled by forces we don't understand, it is hard to take Lockwood's views as seriously as Frank Kermode does.

What view of life does *Wuthering Heights* leave us with?

When Jay Clayton writes about the difficulty of understanding what happens between Heathcliff and Catherine he acutely notes that since we never see "a moment of union" we are left with a "representational void". One result of this void is that critics have tended to fill it in whatever ways they have found most temperamentally or ideologically congenial. Consider, for example, two of the earliest and most influential essays on the novel, by Arnold Kettle and Dorothy van Ghent. In Kettle's Marxist reading, Heathcliff, "the outcast slummy",

> turns to the lively, spirited, fearless girl who alone offers him understanding and comradeship. And she, born into the world of Wuthering Heights, senses that to achieve a full humanity, to be true to herself as a human being, she must associate herself totally with him in his rebellion against the tyranny of the Earnshaws and all that tyranny involves.

In Dorothy van Ghent's Freudian reading,

> *Wuthering Heights* exists for the mind as a tension

between two kinds of reality: the raw, inhuman reality of anonymous natural energies, and the restrictive reality of civilised habits, manners and codes. The first kind of reality is given to the imagination in the violent figures of Catherine and Heathcliff, portions of the flux of nature, children of rock and heath and tempest, striving to identify themselves as human, but disrupting all around them with their monstrous appetite for an inhuman kind of intercourse and finally disintegrated from within by the very energies out of which they are made.

In the one case, the proletarian slummies are being *oppressed* by a tyrannical ruling class; in the other, the unregenerate unconscious is being *suppressed* by the restrictive super-ego.

Arnold Kettle's aggressively politicised warning that readers who will not recognise Heathcliff's "moral force" are "themselves, consciously or not, of the Linton party" is instructively like the critic Keith Sagar's warning that "faint-hearted readers" dare not "leave the padded security of urban and urbane life to confront that which is other, savage and unknowable (perhaps also, if Lockwood is not indeed their double, within themselves)".

All three of these readings, however, are incompatible, though all have elements of truth. Critics often use the works they write about as drunks use a lamppost – for support not illumination – and few novels are easier to do this with than *Wuthering Heights*. But in a novel at once so complex and so puzzling it is wise to be cautious. For one thing, as this guide has tried to show, the romance between Heathcliff and Catherine is not as "romantic" as it might seem; for another, the second half of the book is ignored by many critics, as it is by Hollywood.

My own view is that this is a novel about growing up and about the terrible intensity of feelings which can arise in childhood. Such intensity leads more often to misery than happiness, as is evident in the story of Catherine and Heathcliff. The second Catherine and Hareton are more fortunate; they are lesser beings, less passionate, and more likely to be happy. Given this, as Michael Black has pointed out, the problem for Emily Brontë was preventing the second half from being an anti-climax. "It is meant to be a working out, an appeasement, or a laying to rest of the forces aroused in the first half," he writes:

The Catherine Earnshaw we see at the end of the book is like an exorcised version of the Catherine Earnshaw we see at the beginning, and she is united to a young man who is like an exorcised Heathcliff. For Heathcliff had wanted to brutalise Hareton as Hareton's father had brutalised him. He finds to his puzzlement that this has an unintended effect: Hareton does not resent it; he is not ultimately brutalised at all, nor vengeful, since he has reserves of goodness; and the isolated Catherine comes to love him as the other Catherine had loved Heathcliff. But this time the love is not self-thwarted; the second Catherine learns to subdue her will; in the process she discovers that Hareton is a separate person unlike her projected image of him, and lovable.

The way Catherine sees her forced marriage to the dying Linton through is important in showing her nature. Before the end, Linton says to her: "your kindness has made me love you deeper than if I

WUTHERING HEIGHTS AND MIDDLEMARCH

If we are to consider the novel's "moral implications", as many critics urge, George Eliot's *Middlemarch* serves us better than Charlotte Brontë's apologetic 1850 Preface or Q.D. Leavis's constant but talismanic appeals to "maturity". *Middlemarch*, the most impressively philosophical of all 19th-century English novels, rigorously explores two kinds of egoism – in a way that bears very closely on the difference between Brontë's two Catherines.

Epistemological egoism in unavoidable because every individual just is the centre of his or her universe: hence the famous first sentence of Schopenhauer's *The World as Will and Representation*, "The world is my representation." Epistemological egoism

deserved your love..." – and he dies wishing he'd been worthier of her. Linton is a sickly child conceived in hate and brought up by a strong-willed mother without a father, then taken over by the father in scorn and hate. He is twisted, like Hindley and like Heathcliff, and his life, like theirs, raises what is perhaps the most important question explored in *Wuthering Heights*. As Michael Black expresses it:

> The degree to which we are what we have in native strength, or are what life, especially early life, has twisted us into, like the thorns praying to the sun

then leads, all too easily or naturally, to moral egoism like that of Eliot's Bulstrode, Rosamund Vincy, Casaubon and even young Lydgate, when he chooses his wife as though he were choosing furniture, to adorn his life.

In Chapter 21 of *Middlemarch*, after several chapters that have encouraged the unresisting reader to take a profoundly sympathetic but exclusively Dorothea-centred view of her marital anguish, the reader is suddenly challenged by a momentous change in Dorothea's own attitude to her situation:

> We are all of us born in moral stupidity, taking the world as an udder to feed our supreme selves: Dorothea had early begun to emerge from that stupidity, but yet it had been easier to her to imagine how she would devote herself to Mr. Casaubon than to conceive with that distinctness which is no longer reflection but feeling—an idea wrought back to the directness of sense, like the solidity of

but twisted by the wind, is one of the mysterious issues of the book and it raises the other old question – do we do things 'deliberately'?

Black is recalling here Catherine's defiant words to Nelly when she is justifying her decision to marry Edgar: "I never did anything deliberately." Other critics, notably Q.D. Leavis, take a sterner, more moral view of her actions than she herself (or Michael Black) does. Leavis believes that in this "coherent, deeply responsible novel" the second Catherine's relationship with Hareton is a

objects—that he had an equivalent centre of self whence the lights and shadows must always fall with a certain difference. (21)

Dorothea comes to imagine or conceive how even her emotionally dessicated husband has his own "intense consciousness within him" and his own "small, hungry, shivering self", from which he can never be "liberated". For Eliot, this momentous *moral* advance is only enabled by a corresponding *imaginative* advance, of a kind that we can learn from reading great literature that vividly presents "other consciousnesses". It then makes sense to speak of the moral imagination as something that can release us from what Eliot calls the "moral stupidity" of regarding "the world as an udder to feed our supreme selves" – like Brontë's first Catherine, who can never imagine or conceive even Heathcliff's "equivalent centre of self". This is where the contrast between mother and daughter is most significant – and morally significant ∎

"corrective case history"; the younger Catherine shows herself capable of a maturity which the older Catherine fatally lacks.

Lord David Cecil, in an earlier and very influential essay about *Wuthering Heights*, also sees the second half of the novel as a kind of corrective to the first. His view drew Leavis's formidable scorn – his being a lord didn't help – but his view is not as different from hers as she thinks it is: to suppose that the Cathy-Hareton relationship "corrects" the Catherine-Heathcliff relationship is reassuringly nice and beneficial in terms of conventional morality, but it can't get us past the difficulty that the later relationship is so much less enthralling. Of Heathcliff, Cecil writes that he is not

> as usually supposed, a wicked man voluntarily yielding to his wicked impulses. Like all Emily Brontë's characters, he is a manifestation of natural forces acting involuntarily under the pressure of his own nature. But he is a natural force which has been frustrated of its natural outlet, so that it inevitably becomes destructive; like a mountain torrent diverted from its channel...

Brontë's outlook, Cecil goes on, is not immoral

> but pre-moral. It concerns itself not with moral standards, but with those conditioning forces of life

on which the naïve erections of the human mind that we call moral standards are built up.

It's hard to quarrel with this. Where Cecil is less convincing is in his famous argument that the novel is essentially a carefully patterned weaving of multiple contrasts between storm and calm, as represented respectively by life at the Heights and life at the Grange, and that while Heathcliff and the first Catherine are "the children of storm", the second Catherine and Hareton are "the children of calm". (Offspring of love combine the best qualities of their parents while offspring of hate, like Linton, combine the worst.*) The novel at the end, in this view, with the marriage of Catherine and Hareton, represents a working out of cosmic forces, a restoration of harmony. Much of what Cecil says is perceptive, though his conclusion seems altogether too schematic and sepia-toned.

In his introduction to the 1965 Penguin edition of the novel, David Daiches compares Brontë's view of the world in *Wuthering Heights* with the view to be found in the Gondal poems inspired by her childhood. (Emily was by far the best poet of

*As David Daiches summarises it: "Children of storm mis-mated to children of calm or frustrated in their desire to mate with fellow children of storm are driven to destructive madness; but children of such mis-matings if those mis-matings were made in love and not in hate (e.g. Catherine and Edgar, Hindley and Frances) can themselves mate and restore harmony between opposing elements."

the three sisters.) The comparison is instructive, Daiches argues: the poems, like the novel, reflect Brontë's concern with "the forces of physical passion considered as transcending all human conventions and tending to disrupt all normal morality":

Passion, crime, loss, grief; Byronism and Satanism; curious confusions and transpositions of roles between a dark boy and a fair girl – these run through the Gondal poems, and show an imagination feeding quite wantonly on images of extremes of passion.

To Daiches, the intrusion of Heathcliff into Thrushcross Grange and his vital rapport with the elder Catherine "represents a deeply imagined and vividly presented awareness of some profound and ambiguous force working in man and nature".

The most powerful, the most irresistible, and the most tenacious of forces that reside in the depths of human nature have no relation with the artificial world of civilization and gentility, but they do have a relation to the elemental forces at work in the natural world and also to the impulse to provide the basic elements of a civilized life – fire and food. There is also the recurrent and disturbing suggestion that the depths of man's nature are in some ways alien to him... We might almost say that one of the insights achieved by the novel is that what is most natural is by its very virtue of its being most natural also most unnatural. Man is both at home and not at home in nature. He is capable of perversions and cruelties that are not found in nature, but that is because he is urged on by deep natural forces within him which find themselves at odds with the demands of convention and even of ordinary humanness.

This, it seems to me, comes closer to the truth about *Wuthering Heights* than the more didactic conclusions of Q.D. Leavis or Lord David Cecil. What redeems Heathcliff is his constancy. It is this fidelity – "faithfulness to one's best feelings, regardless of convention," as Michael Black puts it – which makes his nature, and the older Catherine's and Edgar's too, greater than the natures of those who follow them. "Commitment to a feeling," writes Black, "means that you cannot want it to change; that would be a betrayal."

In a novel "so absorbed by the instabilities of identity", says John Matthews, Heathcliff's passion for Catherine involves "a yearning for self-possession" – and in this sense hers for him is similar. Central to the passion of each is a "sense of lack, of an interiority yearning for completion". Their relationship – and the way it is framed by conventional narrators – "rallies our discontent with the oppressive institutions of civilisation that conspire to frustrate their happiness":

> Through their exacting conventionality, Nelly and Lockwood evoke the spectral satisfactions and transgressions that haunt the repressive order of society. Catherine and Heathcliff's love is the ghost of the prohibitions that structure society: it has the air of unspeakably natural passion, even incest, the spaciousness of escape from tyrannous convention, the heedlessness of self-abandon, the dark allure of disease and deathliness.

One grim feature of the first half of *Wuthering Heights* – though not always of its second half – is that its characters seem to be incapable of making what Frank Kermode nicely calls "effective moral choices". Old Earnshaw warps the lives of young Hindley and Catherine when he so suddenly and cruelly transfers his love and affection to the cuckoo-child. The family becomes dysfunctional, if it was not so already. And yet this sudden and appalling cruelty is never explained or presented as something that Earnshaw chooses to do, or even does consciously. And then, as we have seen, it is the same with young Hindley: when he is treated badly he responds badly by turning into a sadistic bully who delights in beating up a child only half his age and size.

Yet Hindley himself can take no real delight – rather than temporary satisfaction or relief – in that development, which ruins his life forever. He becomes a victim of his own cruelty, and remains a warped, vicious creature. Years later, Nelly wonders why her once beloved "playmate", who had seemed to her so much stronger than her third master Edgar Linton, turned into something so much worse. But while the novel takes a more compassionate view than many critics of what happens to Hindley, it never suggests that Hindley had any choice at all about what he became or turned into. The same is true of Heathcliff, much of whose life, as Pauline Nestor puts it, is spent "consumed with frustration, finding himself both literally and figuratively haunted by the endless deferral of satisfaction". Far from "a story of perfect love", Nestor says, the novel can be seen as an exploration of "both the tenacity and the impossibility of such [all-consuming] desire".

Brontë is sceptical about how much can be known, which is evident not least in her remarkable decision to have dual or multiple narrators, sometimes described as "Shakespearean". The comparison seems in place. In *Richard II* we never learn whether or not the King was responsible for the Duke of Gloucester's murder, although so much hinges on that; but then historians can't establish the truth either. In *Henry IV, Part One*, we never know whether or not Mortimer fought with Glendower; Hotspur insists that he did, the King insists that he didn't, the truth remains in limbo. In *Wuthering Heights* we can never be sure whether or not Heathcliff kills Hindley or lets him choke to death, once he has packed Joseph off to fetch the doctor; we hear Nelly, Mr Kenneth, Heathcliff himself and Joseph, without discovering the truth – just as the novel floats the possibility, which strangely never occurs to any of the characters, that Heathcliff might be old Earnshaw's illegitimate son. As we have seen, a similar scepticism about what is true or possible extends to the novel's handling of the supernatural.

No novelist understands completely the springs of his or her imagination, and this seems especially true of Brontë, whose view of life was so unusually dark and mysterious. In her world we are subject to forces we don't understand and can't resist. That the second generation in *Wuthering Heights* turn out to be lesser but happier beings than the first is pure accident; birth and circumstances have shaped them differently; they grow up straighter; they are, quite simply, luckier.

1818 July 30 Emily Jane Brontë born in Thornton, near Bradford in Yorkshire, to Maria Branwell and the Rev. Patrick Brontë. She was the younger sister of Charlotte Brontë and the fifth of six children.

1820 Family moves to Haworth Parsonage

1821 Death of Emily's mother

1824 Emily Brontë enrols at Cowan Bridge School, portrayed by Charlotte as Lowood school in *Jane Eyre*.

1825 Maria Brontë dies of tuberculosis. Charlotte and Emily leave Cowan Bridge School and Elizabeth Brontë dies, also of tuberculosis.

1835 Emily sent home from Roe Head School after feeling very homesick and refusing to speak to anyone but Charlotte.

1836 Emily's first extant poem, *"Will the day be bright or cloudy?"*

1837 Goes to teach at Law Hill School, remains there for around six months.

1838-1842 More than half of Brontë's surviving poems are written

1842 Accompanies Charlotte to Brussels, to M. Heger's school for girls. Returns to Haworth after the death of an aunt.

1845 Charlotte discovers Emily's poetry and convinces her to collaborate a volume of verse

1846 May Poems by Currer, Ellis, and Acton Bell published at the sisters' expense. *Wuthering Heights* finished, begins to make the round of publishers.

1846 September Last complete poem.

1847 Charlotte publishes *Jane Eyre* to critical acclaim. T. C. Newby accepts *Wuthering Heights*, which is published in December.

1848 December 19 Emily Brontë dies

1850 *Wuthering Heights* reissued with a selection of poems and Biographical Notice by Charlotte.

1857 Mrs Gaskell's *The Life of Charlotte Brontë* appears, providing the first published account of the family

1893 Brontë society founded, making it one of the oldest literary societies in the word. Enthusiasts had already begun to make their way to Haworth before Charlotte died in 1855.

1941 Hatfield's edition of *The Complete Poems of Emily Jane Brontë* published.

BIBLIOGRAPHY

Black, Michael, *The Literature of Fidelity*, Chatto & Windus, 1975

Cecil, David, *Early Victorian Novelists*, 1934, republished by Constable 1960

Clayton, Jay, *Romantic Vision and the Novel*, Cambridge University Press, 1987

Coveney, Peter, The Image of Childhood, Penguin, 1967

Daiches, David (ed.), *Wuthering Heights*, Penguin English Library, 1965

Eagleton, Terry, *Myths of Power: A Marxist Study of the Brontes*, Macmillan, 1975

Gaskell, Elizabeth, *The Life of Charlotte Brontë*, 1857, republished by Dent, 1971

Gilbert, Sandra and Gubar, Susan, *The Madwoman in the Attic: the Woman Writer and the Nineteenth-Century Literary Imagination*, Yale University Press, 1979

Jacobs, Naomi, "Gender and Layered Narrative in Wuthering Heights and The Tenant of Wildfell Hall", *The Journal of Narrative Technique*, 1986

Kermode, Frank, *The Classic*, Faber and Faber, 1975

Kettle, Arnold, *An Introduction to the English Novel*, Hutchinson, 1971

Leavis, Q.D., "A Fresh Approach to *Wuthering Heights*", in *Lectures in America*, F.R. Leavis and Q.D. Leavis, Chatto & Windus, 1969

Matthews, John, "Framing in *Wuthering Heights*", Texas Studies in Literature and Language, Spring 1985

McCarthy, Terence, "The Incompetent Narrator of Wuthering Heights", Modern Language Quarterly 42, 1981

Miller, J. Hillis, *The Disappearance of God: Five Nineteenth-Century Writers*, Harvard University Press, 1963

Miller, J. Hillis, *Fiction and Repetition: Seven English Novels*, Harvard University Press, 1982

Miller, Lucasta, *The Brontë Myth*, Jonathan Cape, 2005

Nestor, Pauline (ed.), *Wuthering Heights*, Penguin Classics edition, 1995

Sanger, C. P., *The Structure of Wuthering Heights*, Hogarth Press, 1926

Spacks, *The Female Imagination*, Knopf, 1975

Stoneman, Patsy (ed.), *Wuthering Heights: A reader's guide to essential criticism*, Palgrave Macmillan, 2000

Stoneman, Patsy, *Wuthering Heights, New Casebook series*, Macmillan, 1993

Sutherland, John, *Is Heathcliff a murderer?* Puzzles in 19th-Century Fiction, Oxford University Press, 1996

Van Ghent, Dorothy, *The English Novel: Form and Function*, Harper Torchbooks, 1953

Watt, Ian, *The Victorian Novel: Modern Essays in Criticism*, Oxford University Press, 1971

Winnifith, Tom, *The Brontës and their Background: Romance and Reality*, Macmillan, 1988

INDEX

First published in 2012 by
Connell Guides
Spye Arch House
Spye Park
Lacock
Chippenham
Wiltshire SN15 2PR

10 9 8 7 6 5 4 3 2 1

Picture credits:
p.17 © Corbis
p.37 © Moviestore Collection/ Rex Features
p.45 © Getty
p.57 © Getty
p.71 © Alamy
p.93 © Corbis

A CIP catalogue record for this book is available from the British Library.
ISBN 978-1-907776-24-3
Design © Nathan Burton
Assistant Editor: Katie Sanderson

Printed in Great Britain by Butler Tanner & Dennis

www.connellguides.com